# WORDS

# FROM

# DADDY

# JOE

# WORDS FROM DADDY JOE

FIVE UNFORGETTABLE LESSONS
FROM MY GRANDFATHER
ON LIFE, LEADERSHIP, AND LEAVING A LEGACY

*A Memoir*

## MARK A. GRIDER, ESQ.

*Advantage* | Books

Published by Advantage Books, Charleston, South Carolina.
An imprint of Advantage Media.

ADVANTAGE is a registered trademark, and the Advantage colophon is a trademark of Advantage Media Group, Inc.

Printed in the United States of America.

10  9  8  7  6  5  4  3  2  1

ISBN: 979-8-88750-872-6 (Hardcover)
ISBN: 979-8-89188-104-4 (Paperback)
ISBN: 979-8-89188-105-1 (eBook)

Library of Congress Control Number: 2024920188

Cover design by Matthew Morse.
Layout design by Ruthie Wood.

Advantage Books is an imprint of Advantage Media Group. Advantage Media helps busy entrepreneurs, CEOs, and leaders write and publish a book to grow their business and become the authority in their field. Advantage authors comprise an exclusive community of industry professionals, idea-makers, and thought leaders. For more information go to **advantagemedia.com**.

*This book is dedicated to my grandparents, parents, and wonderful in-laws, who taught me and who continue to model faith, hope, and love. And to my devoted wife for her unwavering support and love. To my son, "Big D," and my cousins, nephews, and nieces—let's together try to always honor God and help people.*

# CONTENTS

ACKNOWLEDGMENTS . . . . . . . . . . IX

INTRODUCTION . . . . . . . . . . . . . . . 1

CHAPTER 1 . . . . . . . . . . . . . . . . . . 9
Be a Soul Man

CHAPTER 2 . . . . . . . . . . . . . . . . . 25
It's All about That Base!

CHAPTER 3 . . . . . . . . . . . . . . . . . 45
People Matter

CHAPTER 4 . . . . . . . . . . . . . . . . 67
Win with Values

CHAPTER 5 . . . . . . . . . . . . . . . . 79
Be Innovative and Creative!

CONCLUSION . . . . . . . . . . . . . . . . 91

APPENDIX I. . . . . . . . . . . . . . . . .93

APPENDIX II . . . . . . . . . . . . . . . . 97

ABOUT THE AUTHOR . . . . . . . . . .99

# ACKNOWLEDGMENTS

To my relatives, in-laws, siblings, friends, and many mentors: Thank you for helping me to lighten up (literally)! Many thanks to Michael Levin and his wonderful team—you are all winners and have a winning culture! Thanks as well to my editor Laura Rashley, who showed me patience, kindness, and dedication. Many thanks to Mrs. Dell' Orco, my seventh- and eighth-grade English teacher, who encouraged me and who declared in class that I was a bright and creative writer and thinker. Thanks to the Saint Louis U. High (SLUH) students (my high school alma mater) for your great feedback and help in making Daddy Joe's lessons resonate with today's culture. Let's continue to do good for others. Finally, thank you to the people who supported and opened great doors of opportunity for me throughout my career and believed in me, so I can now believe in and support others. They have shown me the power of Daddy Joe's lessons, and without those people, I would not be here writing this book.

# INTRODUCTION

This is not your typical faith-based book. This is a "faith-bass" book! *What does that mean?* It simply means that this book has a lot about faith, but it also has a lot of cool bass—it's not stiff and flat. We all enjoy listening to great music, whether it's classical, jazz, rock, or pop, or even popular worship music, Drake, or Taylor Swift. But sometimes, as Meghan Trainor used to say, "It's all about that bass." Sometimes the more bass a song has, the cooler, more harmonious, and enjoyable it is. I believe faith has bass—meaning that the more we harmonize faith into our everyday lives, the cooler, more harmonious, and enjoyable our lives can become. Faith is the backbone of greatness. Join me on this cool "faith-bass" journey, and feel free to turn up the bass as you read!

The goal of this book is to inspire young adults—those in the "critical decade"—between ages sixteen and twenty-six and beyond. I would love to have teenagers and those approaching middle age and beyond join me in practicing (not perfecting—no one is perfect) the foundational principles that enabled my grandfather Daddy Joe to live a life of spiritual goodness and personal greatness. My family is important to me, and so are faith and scripture, which helps me with my strengths and weaknesses, so I'll reference God and certain Bible verses throughout the book—especially as we explore the idea of faith and its impact on our lives—but you'll find that the foundational lessons within this book, and which I share from the Bible, are applicable to anyone who is trying to improve themselves and the world around them, regardless of their religious beliefs. The objective, to borrow from Stephen Covey, is to begin with the end in mind:[1] How do we want our life to end with meaning and purpose? By beginning with the end in mind and focusing on leading our lives from the foundation of our values, we can better serve others and lead fulfilling lives. Daddy Joe exemplified this approach, prioritizing gratitude, humility, and service throughout his life, even as the world around him focused on material success.

My only ask as you read is that you remain open-minded and curious, looking beyond the scripture to connect the meaning with your personal life. To use a silly analogy (there will be plenty throughout the book)—like eleven-time Olympic medalist Simone Biles, we should always focus on the dismount. Just as a gymnast would prior to their routine, we should know or at least think about how we're going to stick the landing.

The key to living a life of meaning is remaining open to what God has in store for us and recognizing that we are neither perfect nor seeking absolute perfection. We are trying to be our best selves by giving and receiving grace, accepting setbacks, and always moving forward.

Oftentimes, I wondered if this book was my "Jerry Maguire" moment. You remember (us more mature readers!): Jerry Maguire was a fictional lawyer and sports agent who was supercompetitive all his life—in sports, law, and business—when suddenly he had a moral epiphany and wrote an intriguing mission statement on how to be more kind, people-centered, and ethical—yet still remain an effective

---

1    Stephen R. Covey, *The 7 Habits of Highly Effective People: Powerful Lessons in Personal Change* (New York: Simon & Schuster, 1989).

agent.[2] Like Jerry, I am admittedly still trying to figure it out. Can we be ultracompetitive in high-powered careers and still find balance? Can we maintain this balance while treating our families, customers, employees, clients, and ourselves with respect?

I use the lessons in this book every day as I strive to reach this balance myself. The following two verses have helped me on this quest and Socratic journey because they reinforce the virtue of reflection:

> **Trust in the Lord and do good (Ps. 37:3, NIV).**

Like Nike's motto, this is simple: *Just do it*! This is about faith in execution.

Another poignant verse that drives this philosophical exploration and causes me to pause and take note of my life is the following:

> **This is what the Lord says: "Stop at the crossroads and look around. Ask for the old, godly way, and walk in it. Travel its path, and you will find rest for your souls." But you reply, "No, that's not the road we want!" (Jer. 6:16, NIV)**

Ultimately, we are all looking for rest for our souls. Through this book, I'm trying to stop and take note of what's surrounding us all. On a personal level, and even on a national and global level, we are at a crossroads. And for those of you who are younger and just starting out on your careers, you're at a personal crossroads of your own as you begin to grow in your capabilities and expand your dreams. We

---

2    *Jerry Maguire*, directed by Cameron Crowe (1996; Culver City, CA: TriStar Pictures).

believe in you, and as many say, "The best is yet to come!" What if we took some of our grandparents' values, experience, and wisdom down from the shelf, dusted them off, and actually put them to use? It's what I've strived to do with this book: to examine Daddy Joe's legacy and how much of my own success I can attribute to how he demonstrated his faith and his values throughout his life. It's a privilege to be able to learn more about ourselves by observing our elders and learning about our ancestors. It enables us to find such solace by remembering what matters. So I ask you for the first time (and it certainly won't be the last): Who's *your* Daddy ... Joe? (It won't be the last pun you get from me in this book either!)

But to take the question seriously for a moment—not everyone has the fortune to know or have relationships with those who came before them, and that's partially why I wanted to write this book. I could have written a business book about my career as a lawyer and working with the White House; maybe I will someday. But I was called to write this memoir first—for my own children and grand-children, who will never have the opportunity to know Daddy Joe themselves except for what I share in these pages and in our home, but also for anyone who might not have their own Daddy Joe in their lives. In this book, we'll talk a lot about relationships and how they shape us. And yes, you can (and should!) apply these lessons to business and leadership, but at its core, this book is about living a life you're proud of, surrounded by people who enable you to be your best, most authentic self. *That's* the book I needed to write first, because that's the foundation that Daddy Joe laid for me growing up. Whether there's a relative, a friend, a mentor, or a teacher or colleague whom you can look up to and trust, I hope there's someone out there whom you'll think of as you read this book and ask yourself, *Who's my Daddy Joe?* If not, well, that's what I'm here for. I'll be with you every step of the way.

I hope this book inspires you to join me on the journey to freedom, success, and peace—the life we deserve!

# Leave Your "But" at Home!

A pro tip to consider when reading this book: Leave your "but" at home! Oftentimes when we read an inspirational story or dare to dream, we add a caveat or a "but." For example, "Yes, I want to go to law school—but ..." or "Yes, I want to pay off my debt—but ..." or "Yes, I want to lose weight—but ..." Stop it! After you read this book, get off the couch and live life. But please, for the sake of your future, leave your but at home!

# Good to Great

Jim Collins, in his 2001 best-selling book *Good to Great: Why Some Companies Make the Leap ... and Others Don't,*[3] described how companies transition from being good companies to great companies and how most companies fail to transition. By no means is this a business book. But like Collins, I thought it would be prudent to consider how we should not settle for an ordinary or good life— perhaps with focus, thoughtful questions, and maybe even a little faith, we can discover a great life! Sometimes getting to a great life requires disruption and changing how we think. As leaders and lawyers, our goal is to help clients see around corners and prepare for the future. (We saw what happened when Blockbuster failed to plan

---

3   Jim Collins, *Good to Great: Why Some Companies Make the Leap ... and Others Don't* (New York: HarperBusiness, 2001).

around Netflix entering the scene—don't fall into the same trap!) If we can exercise this foresight in our own lives, then perhaps we can inspire others to see a brighter future too.

## Digital Transformation versus Reflection

As I write this book, there are numerous conferences regarding AI and digital transformation. As Bill Gates said: "We always overestimate the change that will occur in the next two years and underestimate the change that will occur in the next ten. Don't let yourself be lulled into inaction."[4]

You may ask, "Grider, how can you write a book about purpose and reflection when society and information are moving now at light speed?" My hope is that purpose and reflection are not diametrically opposed to the increasing speed for results, winning, and data and intelligence. I fully understand that we are in a "Win now!" culture—private equity, NIL, NCAA transfer portals, Wall Street, and investors demanding profits. My hope is that this book perhaps slows us down so that we can be better prepared to go fast when the time comes. A friend told me a story that if you're stuck in a boat, you can't just pray—you have to pray and row. Pray and row the boat! As you will see in this book, Daddy Joe did both: he prayed, and he rowed.

## More Cowbell!

Finally, before you begin, I ask you to acknowledge the limitations of this book. In a *Saturday Night Live* sketch with Will Ferrell on April

---

4    Bill Gates, *The Road Ahead* (New York: Viking, 1996), 316.

8, 2000, Christopher Walken shouts, "More cowbell! More cowbell!"[5] (A classic, must-see skit!)

Similarly, readers have yelled out to me, "More Daddy Joe! More Daddy Joe!" While I wish that I could include "more Daddy Joe" and his life, I ask you to please accept that I could not cover everything in this book. Perhaps if this book finds success and helps others achieve personal growth, I will write another with "more Daddy Joe," or even start a Daddy Joe podcast![6]

## Five Unforgettable Lessons from My Grandfather on Life, Leadership, and Leaving a Legacy

### Be a Soul Man

### It's All about That Base

### People Matter

### Win with Values

### Be Innovative and Creative

---

5   "More Cowbell," *Saturday Night Live*, season 25, episode 16, directed by Beth McCarthy-Miller, featuring Christopher Walken and Will Ferrell, aired April 8, 2000, on NBC.

6   Throughout the book, all names, with the exception of well-known celebrities, sports figures, and Daddy Joe, have been changed. Some of the stories in this book are memories of memories told over generations and are shared here in the way that family lore is shared.

# CHAPTER 1

## Be a Soul Man

*Daddy Joe's Guide for Life*

> *He who wins souls is wise.*
>
> *—Proverbs 11:3 (NKJV)*
>
> *He restores my soul. He leads me in paths of righteousness.*
>
> *—Psalms 23:3 (ESV)*

In the 1960s and 1970s, there was a simple but significant change in basketball that revolutionized the sport. In 1986, the NCAA adopted the three-point shot into the official game rules. Basketball evolved from players darting around the court at high speed to players strategically standing outside the perimeter, trying to rack up a higher number of points with one shot.

The three-point shot added more suspense to a heated game (maybe that's why they call it March Madness). Teams trailing close

WORDS FROM DADDY JOE

behind their competitors now had a better chance of closing the gap if they focused on the elusive shot. Eventually the three-point shot made its way to the NBA and WNBA, and it is now a staple of basketball and has disrupted and changed the way basketball is played (thank you, Steph Curry, Sabrina Ionescu, Ray Allen, Caitlin Clark, Luka Dončić, and many others—see the 2015, 2017, 2018, and 2022 NBA Champion Golden State Warriors "Splash Brothers" if you don't believe me). The three-point shot, which many sportscasters call the "trifecta," is a game changer. It opens the court to new possibilities, can disrupt the opponent's momentum by silencing the crowd, encourages players to refine their skill sets, and creates more life and excitement for participants and spectators alike.

In many ways, the three-point shot reminds me of my grandfather Daddy Joe. When my grandfather passed away at the age of ninety-two, he had been married for over seventy years. He had three beautiful children, ten grandchildren, and three great-grandchildren. Daddy Joe left our family with a profound spiritual legacy that inspires us to pursue lives defined by purpose and passion.

Over one hundred years ago, Daddy Joe was a game changer for our family and his surrounding community. He opened a new world of opportunities for his children and following generations by choosing to live fearlessly. Like the effect of a three-point shot in a crowded stadium, Daddy Joe breathed new life and enthusiasm into his surrounding community. I remember sitting as a young man in Daddy Joe's church on a particularly hot Chicago summer morning when a thought skidded across my mind. While watching him deliver a charismatic message to the congregation that revered and loved him, it occurred to me that Daddy Joe must have a secret—a strategy of some kind—that lifted him from his humble beginnings to being a masterful builder of great things throughout his lifetime.

*What was it?* I wondered. A few years passed before I finally discovered his secret weapon: the Trifecta. Now I'm excited to share it with you.

Coincidentally, Daddy Joe believed in the power of three and lived his life according to three staple virtues, "the Trifecta": faith, perseverance, and humility.

In the 1940s, trying to achieve the American Dream was challenging for many, and for some, it was an exceptionally difficult and risky feat, to say the least. Nevertheless, Daddy Joe made the courageous decision to uproot his life in Mississippi and venture to the foreign territory of Illinois in search of a better life for his family. Through a determined work ethic and unwavering devotion to the Trifecta, Daddy Joe not only survived the transition, but he also prospered in the process.

I recall a 1950s family story about Daddy Joe and Mother (as we lovingly called his beautiful, healthy wife—my grandmother) driving through the country with their young children in the car. They stopped to use the restroom and get soda and perhaps candy. Because Daddy Joe was a person of color and not from the area, three local individuals ordered him to go behind the back of the store. Knowing that things would not end well, Daddy Joe distracted the men and helped his family run to the car and escape. They drove off without the soda and candy, but at least they were safe! Daddy Joe forgave—and unfortunately, I also realized where I may have inherited my high knees and speed for college football!

Daddy Joe was determined to send all three of his children to school, and this determination is clearly evident from his work ethic. Daddy Joe worked hard as a porter at a Chicago pie company for over thirty years. On the side, he sold eggs, did other odd jobs, and miraculously had time to serve as leader and pastor in his community's church. Although he worked hard at multiple jobs at a time, Daddy Joe gave his full attention and efforts to each task. Daddy Joe was a hardworking family man his entire life, working at Fasano Pies in Chicago until he retired.

Daddy Joe was a powerful and inspirational leader because his vision was grounded in something greater than himself. The foundation of his character rested in his faith, and the life structure he built was centered on the Trifecta: faith, perseverance, and humility. These pillars enabled Daddy Joe to live a vibrant, impactful life well into his nineties. Daddy Joe was prosperous in the greatest sense of the word—his life was rich in fulfilling relationships, material and physical well-being, influence, and joy. He is a brilliant example of what life can amount to when lived purposefully.

## Faith

When Daddy Joe left for Chicago in the midst of the pre–civil rights era, he faced many unknown factors. Leaving his family and journeying north required courage. From where does such courage come? What sets apart those with the audacity to follow their inner voice from those who remain stationary on their couches, dreaming of what could be, while their lives go largely unlived?

That courage is faith, and Daddy Joe had it. He believed in something greater than himself. He knew he was never walking through life alone. There was always a higher presence, knowledge, and power he could rely on moving by his side and through him. This faith allowed him to take risks and pursue greatness with confidence and courage.

Faith is a function of belief and hope. Daddy Joe believed the hand of God was orchestrating life on his behalf. This unwavering belief carried him through every hardship, setback, and triumph life dealt him. Daddy Joe built the empire of his legacy on faith and blessed hundreds in the process, including me. He taught me to act on faith and trust in a plan greater than my own understanding. Regardless of whether you're religious, everyone can benefit from acknowledging some things are out of our control and that by "trusting the process," we can accept and grow from things that we perceive don't go our way.

I relied on his example over twenty years ago, when I felt called to leave my life in Missouri to work on Capitol Hill. Many well-intentioned friends and relatives questioned my decision to leave. I was often asked, "Are you sure you want to leave your life here? What about your family and friends?" There were moments when I felt tempted to say, "Maybe you're right. I think I'll just stay in Missouri."

Fortunately, I landed an opportunity to meet John Danforth, an extremely faith-filled and wise US senator, who imparted wisdom to me that altered my life trajectory. When I revealed my reservations about moving to Washington, DC, he became very serious, looked me squarely in the eyes, and asked, "Why hide your talents under a rock, Mark?[7] You are a leader. You've got to get in the game and make decisions. Follow your heart. Follow your nose."

After that meeting, I got on my knees and prayed. It was time to cultivate faith in the talents and opportunities with which I was blessed. I needed to follow in Daddy Joe's footsteps and trust the stirrings of my heart. *I needed faith.*

Of course, faith doesn't mean taking rash or unplanned action. You must be strategic and smart when making decisions. Faith means

---

7    He was referring to the New Testament parable, found in Matthew 25:14–30, of the servant who was too scared to invest in the talents given to him, so he hid the talents in the ground.

trusting in your well-thought-out plans and recognizing that your decisions are valid. Having faith means believing that every event in your life, every choice you make, is done for a reason, and that your faith works behind the scenes on your behalf. It is a belief in an invisible contract, knowing that if you do your part, the rest will fall into place.

Moving to Washington, DC, was one of the best decisions of my life. Senator John Ashcroft, another prominent faith-guided senator on Capitol Hill, mentored me (as well as other staff and DC friends) while I worked for him as a legislative aide and then a legislative assistant. He gave me the opportunity to serve people so that I could make an impact in my community and home state. I experienced firsthand how truly miraculous it is when life opens up after you approach it from a service standpoint and offer your gifts to support and inspire others. From that point on, my life, achievements, and relationships blossomed, because I was working with a leader who was centered, balanced, and wise.

With the same faith that moved mountains in Daddy Joe's life, I was able to start building my own legacy.

## Perseverance

My life—and perhaps yours—has been littered with setbacks. Life fluctuates, much like the stock market: for every few highs, there's been at least one low. I experienced my first major setback during my freshman year of college. (I won't even talk about my awkward high school days.)

I was attending an NCAA Division II school on a football scholarship at Truman State University. Football was my passion and life, and my team was my family (or so it seemed). I even had wild dreams of trying out for the NFL (no, not the National Federation of Librarians).

Disappointment struck midway through my freshman year preseason when an injury forced me onto the sidelines. I was heart-broken. *How could God have let this happen to me?* I thought. This wasn't the way I envisioned my college football career unfolding. I couldn't fathom how getting hurt, and consequently stuck on the bench cheering my teammates on, could possibly work out in my favor, but it did.

During my recovery, I often thought about Daddy Joe and the perseverance he employed to push through life challenges. I realized I had two options: I could pack up my bags and go home, or I could persevere through this hardship and trust that God would work every-thing out in my favor. My older sister sent me a Bible verse, which I put up on my dorm room wall: "All things work together for good for those who love God and are called according to His purpose" (Rom. 8:28, NIV). This powerful verse gave me the courage I needed to persevere that year, and believe it or not, that verse has grounded me over the many years as a trial lawyer and in corporate America.

What I couldn't see with my shortsighted vision was that my life's purpose was much greater than football. Being put on the sidelines my freshman year led to a strong performance in the classroom instead of on the field. My grade point average jumped that first year, and I ended up being named to the dean's list, which set the academic precedent for my remaining collegiate years.

My injury, which led to better grades, also indirectly opened the door for me to work at the state capitol in Jefferson City, Missouri, during my senior year—for Senator J. B. "Jet" Banks, a well-known African American Saint Louis politician, who was the senate majority floor leader at the time (many thanks to the dean at the university who suggested this opportunity for me).

Through his mentorship, I learned even more about the value of hard work and perseverance. Little did I know these challenging circumstances were preparing me for a future career in law and public policy, along with other leadership endeavors.

My freshman-year injury, as difficult as it was, deepened my faith. It taught me the importance of resiliency and persevering forward, trusting the process, even if the path is winding and difficult. As the Saint Louis federal judge Booker Shaw told me, "Sometimes in life, you take two steps back to go four steps forward."

My hometown of Saint Louis is also home to a little-known story of perseverance that proved one of the most important stories in American history. Today, we remember Ulysses S. Grant as the commanding general of the US Army in the Civil War, the two-term president of the United States, and the relentless crusader for civil rights and racial equality. But his life was not always so heroic. In fact, if you met him at any point in his adult life before the Civil War, you might consider him a failure.

Despite success as an officer in the Mexican-American War, his alcoholism consumed him at the end of the war, and he never found his footing in civilian life. He repeatedly fell victim to scammers, losing his meager life savings in Ponzi schemes and ill-fated business ideas. Eventually, he was unable to even provide for his family. After he failed to make a living in his hometown of Galena, Illinois, his wife and children had no choice but to move in with in-laws. As if the shame of his failure to provide for his own family were not enough, it was politically and socially awkward—Grant was an abolitionist Republican, but his in-laws were slaveholding Southerners.

Meanwhile, Grant moved into a spare room owned by his wife's cousin in Saint Louis, without heat or sustenance. He continued searching for work, contacting friends, and clawing his way into society. Even during his season of deepest shame, however, Grant read voraciously. He pored over newspapers, studied maps, and implored his friends to consider the risks of war. He watched the rise of the Confederacy and had the foresight to understand its implications. And he was right.

Once war broke out, army leaders remembered Grant's skills in the Mexican-American War and called him back to service. His deft leadership, clever logistics, and swift decision-making led the Union Army on a romp through the Western Theater, defeating Confederate armies and setting the stage for his final confrontation as general-in-chief of all Union forces with General Robert E. Lee's Army of Virginia.

His meteoric rise to the top of the army, where he won swift and full support of leaders, including Secretary of War Edwin Stanton and President Abraham Lincoln, baffled his friends back in Saint Louis. Could this really be the same man they knew in Missouri? The nearly homeless and completely feckless quiet soul with the sad eyes and the thick beard?

When I face a daunting challenge in life, I think back to my home in Saint Louis, where I played football and met Senator Banks, and I remember the challenges General Grant faced only blocks away. Today, my office is a five-minute walk away from the White House, where Grant eventually lived. But Grant never dreamed of that fate when he shivered in a cold room in Saint Louis. He could have folded his cards and accepted failure. He could have succumbed to his clinical addiction to alcohol, abandoned his family, and declared himself a victim of the world's cruelties.

But he rejected that temptation. He kept studying, working, and focusing on his strengths. He knew that a time would come when he would be called to rise to the occasion—that he was being prepared, as the Jewish and Christian traditions say about Esther, "for such a time as this." He persevered.

Life will undoubtedly give you setbacks. The goal is to learn from them. I was once told in my career that "setbacks are a setup for a comeback." I now see this as true. I learned that when you fail, always fail forward. Every pass you throw isn't going to be a touchdown, and there will be many interceptions and plenty of injuries. When you persevere through challenges, believing that there is a game plan far greater than the play you've been practicing on the field, you open your life to wonder and miracles. You open your life to greatness. I believe that *greatness* is achieved once one engages in character development and service to others.

# Humility

Humility comes last in the Trifecta, because it is the final ingredient that allows us to transcend our weaknesses and self-imposed limitations. Humility is the willingness to acknowledge our imperfections and to accept help when we need it. A friend once said that humility also gives us the courage to move forward, instead of getting so down on ourselves that we just give up when we reach setbacks.

Daddy Joe understood something that many leadership gurus do not. We often evaluate leaders based on their charisma, charm, or public speaking. But Daddy Joe never considered adding those to the Trifecta. Let me explain why he was correct to favor humility over these sexier alternative traits.

Although humility transcends faiths, Daddy Joe was a preacher. He knew that when Jesus gave his famous Sermon on the Mount, the very first words out of his mouth were "blessed are the poor in spirit, for theirs is the kingdom of heaven" (Matt. 5:3, NIV). The phrase "poor in spirit" has nothing to do with personal finances; it means *humility*.[8] It's the opposite of self-righteousness. That's why the Jewish prophet Micah boiled down the life of faith to an admonition "to act justly, to love mercy, and to walk humbly with your God" (Mic. 6:8).

But humility is not just for preachers like Daddy Joe. Humility has shaped great leaders throughout history. After reflecting on Ulysses S. Grant, we can look to another great American general-turned-president: Dwight D. Eisenhower. We celebrate General Eisenhower for leading the Invasion of Normandy—the Allied culmination of Operation Overlord, which ultimately freed France from Nazi control. History remembers the overwhelming success of D-Day on June 6, 1944, as a military victory that catapulted Eisenhower into being a global hero and future president. But as late as the day before the invasion, that victory was hardly assured.

The Normandy Invasion presented daunting challenges of weather, logistics, and heavy opposing firepower. Eisenhower knew he could be sending 160,000 men to their deaths, and he did not ignore the gravity of that decision. But unlike many leaders who have passed blame for failure and littered their decisions with excuses and caveats, Eisenhower was ready to accept them with humility.

---

8    I'm no scholar of biblical languages, but I understand that the Greek phrase in this verse, *ptochos*, refers to someone who bows. The prophet Isaiah taught that God looks on the person who is "humble and contrite in spirit and trembles at my word" (Isa. 66:2, NIV). So Jesus's "poor in spirit" do not march proudly before God, as if they have something to teach him; they are humble before him and willing to listen to his word. That sounds a lot like someone who says, "God, I'm open" and "I'm obedient," which are lessons we will discuss in later chapters.

After Eisenhower watched paratroopers depart on the night of June 5, 1944, he sat down to write a speech he prayed he would never need to give:[9]

> Our landings in the Cherbourg-Havre area have failed to gain a satisfactory foothold and I have withdrawn the troops. **My decision to attack** at this time was based upon the best information available. The troops, the air and the Navy did all that bravery and devotion to duty could do. **If any blame or fault attaches to the attempt, it is mine alone.**

In his handwritten draft, you can see that Eisenhower crossed out his initial words "this particular operation," replacing that clinical language with a personal assumption of responsibility: "my *decision*." Eisenhower had the humility to recognize his own fallibility and the character to own up to it. In the words of Harry S. Truman, my fellow Missourian and President Eisenhower's predecessor, "The buck stops here!"

When we understand that great leaders adopt a posture of humility and servant leadership, we realize that "humility" is not just a word for pastors and generals. It's part of the Trifecta for guiding our own everyday lives. As an added benefit, everyone is drawn to a person with humility. C. S. Lewis wrote that if you meet a truly humble person, you are drawn to them in a way that faux-charismatic leaders cannot replicate:[10]

---

9   Richard Nixon, "Statement on the Death of General Eisenhower," online by Gerhard Peters and John T. Woolley, The American Presidency Project, https://www.presidency.ucsb.edu/node/238774.

10   C. S. Lewis, *Mere Christianity* (New York: HarperOne, 2001), chapter 8.

> Do not imagine that if you meet a really humble man
> he will be what most people call 'humble' nowadays:
> he will not be a sort of greasy, smarmy person, who
> is always telling you that, of course, he is nobody.
> Probably, all you will think about him is that he seemed
> a cheerful, intelligent chap who took a real interest in
> what you said to him. If you do dislike him, it will be
> because you feel a little envious of anyone who seems
> to enjoy life so easily. He will not be thinking about
> humility: he will not be thinking about himself at all.

We all require improvement and guidance in different areas of life. To call back to my days of playing football, it takes humility to say, "You know what, Coach? I need to come out of the game for a bit. I need to get some help." Or to ask your manager for feedback or development, as another example. Or to hire an executive coach or a personal counselor. Unfortunately, we've been socially conditioned to magnify our strengths and hide our weaknesses. This doesn't serve us; rather, it tremendously blocks sustainable success that can impact future generations.

I'm learning to not let the spotlight on my achievements keep me from admitting where I still need to experience growth and improvement. There are a lot of successful athletes, politicians, students, and businesspeople who have risen to great heights in one specific area of their lives. Because of their success, and the outward pressure to be perfect, these individuals are often too embarrassed to seek help when they need it.

Seeking help by reflecting on our foundational principles and reaching out to others for support is the ultimate act of humility and an emblem of strength. Of course, it's intimidating to open a closet piled high with secrets that we don't want to address. Yet sorting through the mess and letting go of the dead weight that's been inhibiting our growth is the ultimate act of liberation. Humility makes it possible.

No one is perfect—not even Daddy Joe. One of his greatest character flaws was that he had a sharp temper. However, he didn't let his temper take over his life. He found the humility to step back from his irritation and to accept my grandmother's guidance and compassion-filled point of view. He could admit he wasn't always right and that he didn't always have the answers. Mother would often say, "Joe, calm down and listen!" And listen he did.

This willingness to be humble and open to outside points of view is what made my grandparents' marriage so formidable and strong. They were a powerful team, because they discovered the truth in the old African proverb, "If you want to go fast, go alone. If you want to go far, go together." Hand in hand and side by side, my grandparents built a marriage and family spanning seventy years—an amazing accomplishment, considering the hard work it takes (we all experience the effort it takes to build and keep together a loving marriage and family in the busyness of today's culture!).

All relationships, partnerships, and pursuits of self-growth require humility and the willingness to accept help and outside guidance. I've heard some people say they can make a lot of changes in their lives, but becoming humbler isn't one of them. Listen: if Daddy Joe could cultivate humility and cooperation despite falling into occasional fits of heated rage rivaling those of a charging bull, surely all of *us* can strive toward having more humility in our lives, regardless of any imperfection we believe stands in our way. But it's a daily process. The more I remind myself to be humble, the more blessed I feel.

# The True Nature of Success

It's time for our culture to expand its definition of success. A successful life means more than building a great company or a career. It's more than amassing millions of dollars too. A successful life is a balanced one in which relationships, health, and the joy of contributing to our communities are cultivated and valued.

As a mentor, I encourage those I coach to reflect on their values and the legacy they want to leave behind. In a world that often prioritizes salary and climbing the corporate ladder, it's crucial to remember that true success lies in serving others and staying true to oneself.

Daddy Joe understood this wisdom; his life is a testament to the power of leading with gratitude, humility, and a commitment to service. He realized that a prosperous life demands inner conviction, a strong framework, and strategic planning. To lead lives that surpass conventional limits, we must put aside our egos and build something greater together. We must build toward achieving faith, perseverance, and humility. We should "shoot the Trifecta."

# Putting Words into Action: Reflection Questions

Grab a notebook, pen, or even a basketball! It's time to shoot around and practice our trifecta (the power of three)!

## FAITH

Do the images, people, and entertainment with which you surround yourself spark and uplift your faith? Do they inspire you to be a better person? Do you have a way to believe in your value as a person outside of status symbols and achievements? If the answer is no, how can you change this? List three inspirational words or images that revive your faith, trust in others, and self-confidence. Display them and revisit them often.

## PERSEVERANCE

Think of a time when you were in a challenging situation and felt like giving up. Maybe you were failing a class or had been rejected for a job. Consider the obstacles and excuses that may have held you back. How did you push through it?

The ancient Roman writer Vegetius wrote: "In times of peace, prepare for war." What challenges lie ahead of you that you need to prepare for? Can you anticipate where you will need the quality of perseverance?

Finally, identify three cultural, historic, or current life events that model the best ways to keep going. Record them for future reference and revisit them in difficult times.

## HUMILITY

In which relationships and situations could you bring more humility? In what areas can you improve your willingness to see another's point of view? Where in your life could you use a coach or mentor? Whom in your life can you turn to for help at any time? Gather the contact information for these people and add them to your address book, mobile contacts, or digital favorites. How do you ensure you maintain these relationships?

# CHAPTER 2
# It's All about That Base!

*Building a Foundation*

Ever get a song or ad jingle stuck in your head? In 2015, I think I had the song "All about That Bass"—a pop music chart-topper by Meghan Trainor—playing in my head literally all year long: "You know I'm all about that bass, 'bout that bass, no treble." It became my personal anthem when working out at the gym! I kid, but only to a certain extent. If you assess your life, it's fairly obvious that it really is all about that *base* we establish for ourselves.

The quality of your life circumstances—whether you have healthy or dysfunctional relationships, a fulfilling career, or a frustrating job—is determined by the quality of the base you create. I think of self-care as your first foundational base. It's the foundation of your career, relationships, and all you do.

There are three main components of self-care: soul, mind, and body. On top of this self-care base are (1) relationships, (2) your "life business plan" or career, and (3) beautification.

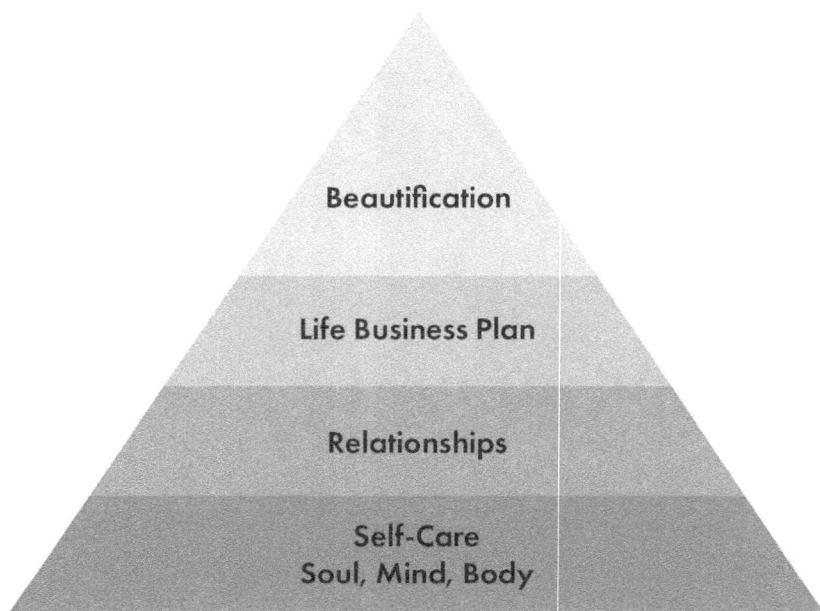

Beautification

Life Business Plan

Relationships

Self-Care
Soul, Mind, Body

If you've ever seen Maslow's Hierarchy of Needs, which places psychological safety as the foundation of the pyramid, this may look familiar to you. Self-care of the soul and mind absolutely improves our psychological safety, and self-care of the body—getting physically stronger, learning your body's chemical reactions to certain environments, etc.—goes a long way in this regard too. Taking care of our whole selves—soul, mind, body—allows us to know ourselves better, which in turn allows us to have more faith in ourselves and our decision-making. Researchers at the National Health Service (NHS) have studied this theory, analyzing the needs and behaviors of elite performers, and found that employee health is directly linked to performance and productivity levels.[11] Healthy employees, in both mind and body, consistently showed higher levels of contributions

---

11  Marco Hafner et. al, "Employee Engagement in the NHS," *RAND Health Quarterly* 1, no. 9 (June 15, 2020): 3. PMID: 32742745.

and engagement. Essentially, from muscle to mind, a healthy body is more than relevant to business performance; it's essential.

Unless you want your career and relationships to constantly topple over, they need to be supported by hearty self-care habits and mindsets. Sometimes, though it seems counterintuitive, putting yourself first can help you serve others and achieve the other goals you may have in life.

## Working from the Inside Out

I've found that a lot of people want to build their lives from the outside in. Instead of focusing on creating a strong, expansive foundation that can uphold great ambitions, sometimes we can spend our time obsessing over small, external, cosmetic details.

Too many people believe happiness and fulfillment are only obtained through a job title or by accruing a lot of wealth. Contrary to what we tell ourselves, getting that new corner office won't fundamentally revolutionize our lives. The happiness that these changes evoke is short-lived. These gratifications are minor in the long run because they don't substantially change the core of who we are for the better.

If we want to create real change in our day-to-day experiences—change that can potentially impact others and grow our lives to heights beyond our wildest expectations—we must first address the foundation on which we live. It's time to strengthen our base ... because it is truly all about that base!

## Soul

As a college athlete, I trained for the football season all year round (even though I played "left out" on the team—literally, I was left out when the bus was heading to the game!). Although the team wasn't competing on the field 365 days a year, we were expected to remain strong and fit at all times. We needed to be in a constant state of physical preparedness so that when the time came, we could execute the game plan and win!

I've found that our souls require the same preparedness and discipline. Just as we must move our bodies regularly if we want to remain healthy and strong, we must exercise our souls consistently if we want to be powerful and wise.

Exercising our inner life a few times a year simply won't cut it. This inconsistency leaves us spiritually flabby. In this state, we can't see our life's bigger picture. We're robbed of the ability to focus effectively on what counts, which leads to an outlook riddled with confusion and indecision. No one wants to be in such a state.

## Standing in Spirit

To stand powerfully in our lives and make decisions aligned with our priorities and goals, we need to connect with our spirit—we need to be healthy from the inside out!

A healthy soul transcends fear and helps us soar above life's storms. Visiting the nation's capital is a wonderful thing. If you're able to visit, you'll notice that in the Capitol and around Washington, DC, are representations of the bald eagle. The Founding Fathers chose it as the national bird in 1782, symbolizing the young country's pride and strength. The Great Seal of the United States, with the bald eagle at its center, is a symbol that holds various meanings as a totem of inspiration for US leadership. When leaders and individuals are having tough times, we can look to the bald eagle and remember how it locks its wings and soars above the storms of life. John Ashcroft, a former

Missouri senator and mentor of mine, even wrote an inspirational song: "Let the Eagle Soar."

Like an eagle, we can remain serene and at peace during times of turmoil because we have a vision and faith that allow us to see the bright horizon just beyond the clouds. Day-to-day concerns loosen their tight grip over our lives as we practice connecting with ourselves and trusting what we believe in.

This perspective repositions our focus and heartens our overall sense of well-being and personal power. It also helps us realize that our actions and decisions have consequences; they can have powerful impacts on our children, livelihood, legacy, and community.

Daddy Joe made a lot of decisions based on the impacts they would have on his family, friends, and community. A memorable example involves Daddy Joe's love for chewing tobacco. Back then nobody really knew how bad it was; it was just a habit a lot of folks had. One Saturday afternoon, we were all over at Daddy Joe and Mother's house in Chicago. I walked up to Daddy Joe as he stood on the front porch. Of course, at about seven years old, I wore little blue shorts and white socks pulled up to my calves—I thought I was looking pretty cool. Anyway, a neighbor walking by greeted Daddy Joe. As he turned to return the greeting and spit out the chewing tobacco, it landed all over my white tube socks. He didn't even know I was back there! Mother was hysterical and shouted, "Joe, you spit on your grandson!" There I stood, shocked, with spittle on my knee and on my tube socks—it looked like a backward brown Nike swoosh draining into my shoes! Although it was an accident, I don't recall seeing Daddy Joe ever chewing tobacco again. I'm sure he was embarrassed, and perhaps this incident was a catalyst to kick the tobacco habit, or so I'm told. That's just the type of person he was—he never wanted to do anything that could hurt others.

Daddy Joe was always careful about what he said and did because he knew the impacts his actions had on those around him. From this realization, we can walk with purpose. We can cultivate the values of integrity, compassion, and kindness—attributes that emanate from the goodness of our souls. These values serve us in all areas of life, from our interpersonal relationships to the establishment of a strong corporate culture.

## Bed Skirts and the Golden Rule

My first summer job during college was a managerial internship at JCPenney (many thanks to the manager, who took the time to teach me business skills). I was in charge of the bedding section. That's right: while my football teammates were out cutting grass or laying shingles that hot, sticky summer, I was learning more about bed skirts and pillow shams than I care to remember! (This was all before Jeff Bezos and Amazon!)

While I expected to learn the intricacies of bedding, housewares, business, and balance sheets during the internship, I didn't expect to discover the importance of strong values in corporate culture. This discovery changed my life.

Up until then, I never saw a direct relationship between my spiritual walk and business success. James Cash Penney, the founder of JCPenney, showed me otherwise. He used the Golden Rule as the cornerstone of his managerial practices: "Do unto others as you would have them do to you." He founded JCPenney on this principle and even named his first retail store the Golden Rule. He was a staunch advocate of honesty, integrity, and kindness in business and incorporated these values into the culture of his retail empire.[12] This spiritual model of business success reaped him tremendous financial benefits.

Penney's legacy, as well as Daddy Joe's, profoundly impacted the way I approach my career. Both men helped me realize that I don't have to walk into the office with a perspective of "me versus them"— that kindness, integrity, and success go hand in hand. In fact, they often flow better when all three elements are present and feeding off each other. This is the spiritual law of success.

Oftentimes, when we enter corporate jobs, we carry a dog-eat-dog mentality or a zero-sum mindset. It's a conviction that says, "I have to win today at any cost, no matter who or what I have to trample to reach the finish line first." But when we're connected with ourselves and our beliefs, winning and losing don't carry the same weight. Our self-worth isn't connected to what we do; it's in who we are!

I believe a winning ethical culture can be built on the principles of treating people fairly and ensuring strong accountability while creating shareholder profits. Daddy Joe and James Cash Penney understood this principle, and they used it to build fruitful lives and lasting legacies. You and I can do the same.

## Feeding Your Soul

Tapping into your soul is a function of self-control and discipline. If you want to feel the impacts of your spirituality, you must connect with it daily.

I'm reminded of the one and only night I shared a room with Daddy Joe and Mother. To save costs (Daddy Joe was frugal and insisted on paying with cash), I, along with Daddy Joe, Mother, and

---

12   "Defining the Golden Rule," JCPenney.com, accessed March 2019, https://www. jcpenney.com/penneypointers/defining-the-golden-rule/.

other family members, ended up rooming together during a Chicago family reunion while I was in college. As I got ready for bed, sleeping on the comfy and smelly hotel pullout couch, I saw an image that remains with me: on the other side of the hotel room, Daddy Joe tenderly lowered his old eighty-six-year-old frame to his knees. He folded his hands in front of his chest, and he prayed. It was immediately clear that this was his evening ritual and was just as important as brushing his teeth or putting on his pajamas. It was his personal method for building a spiritual base, or perhaps he was just praying for the White Sox, Cubs, or Bears! I guess it doesn't matter because at least he was taking the time to get on his knees and pray.

I was touched by the simplicity and reverence in the ritual. From that day forward, I've sought to create my own rituals for filling up my soul and building a strong base, something that you can easily do for yourself too. Check out the reflection section at the end of this chapter for some ideas on getting started building your strong base.

## The Four P's

Our family has its own method we like to call the "four P's":

1. Pause

2. Pray

3. Peace

4. Praise

Even though the name is a colloquial reminder of practicing humility, living your best life by the four P's is a powerful spiritual tool. It requires discipline and devotion. I found that the four P's can help me, and others, whether responding to an accusatory email or dealing with difficult personalities (and perhaps the four P's can help us all before tweeting!). Nevertheless, when you stick with the game, you reap tremendous rewards, contentment, and peace beyond our understanding.

I like to use the four P's when I need to make an important decision. Or sometimes it's a great method to get started in the morning. I pause and take a moment to reflect. It's freeing and humbling to acknowledge the awe of getting to live another day, to be able to say, "Thank you for today."

I like to allow this offering of gratitude to lead me into prayer. *If prayer isn't for you, then consider replacing the second *P* with "Plea." Like prayer, pleas are earnest requests to validate the faith you're building that everything will happen as it should. It can take the form of meditation, journaling, etc. Prayer is simply the vehicle that I personally find the most fulfillment in. After prayer, I check in with my inner peace. The peace component of the four P's is simply listening to your soul. What do you feel? Do you feel good or bad about a decision you have made or are about to make?

Lastly, praise is showing even more gratitude for our life. Happiness is directly linked to the amount of gratitude present in our lives. Praise allows us to expand our joy while acknowledging what life has offered us. It's an extremely powerful way to start the day and make decisions that move us toward success.

## Creating a Powerful Mind

Choosing to make our beds every morning isn't necessarily a fun task, but we do it anyway—at least, we hopefully do. We put in the effort to pull up our sheets and straighten out the pillowcases because it adds value and order to our days.

Our beds aren't the only part of our lives that need to be made every morning. Our minds require the same attention. As my parents always told me when I was a kid, "You must make up your mind every morning that today is going to be a good day." They would shout, "This is the day the Lord has made! We will rejoice and be glad in it!" It was a good thing I was a morning person.

This requires a conscious decision. It's up to us to declare that, regardless of what happened yesterday or the day before, we're going to mine all the joy, blessings, and fulfillment out of each moment to come.

Daddy Joe always started his day saying, "Good morning." When he said this phrase, he literally meant it was going to be a *good* morning.

Adopting such an empowered mindset, like Daddy Joe's, allows us to take control over our experiences. I find that stating positive declarations can positively impact how I feel and others around me. Instead of being reactive or playing victim, we can become drivers rather than passengers. In this way, you have to lose in order to win, meaning that you have to let go of those old mindsets and behaviors. You cannot fully live in a place of empowerment without doing so. Lose those bad habits, and you'll win back more than you likely ever planned. By declaring positive, affirmative statements, like "Good morning," we can take ownership of our lives and how we feel and act. Doing so means that we set our agenda with intention rather than relying on other circumstances to decide our lives or futures for us.

Creating a clean, positive mind requires strategy. My favorite tool is *awareness*. Rather than blindly going through the motions of the day, try to be conscious of the thoughts consistently running through your mind. And if you don't like the thoughts, work hard to change them. We are 100 percent accountable for our thoughts. It's far too easy to get sucked into a funnel of negativity if we're not consciously monitoring our mental activity. It's up to us to be diligent gatekeepers of our minds. You may have heard before, "Our thoughts become our reality." We must only allow positive ideas through the gates.

In 2010, the Washington Wizards basketball team selected one of the fastest point guards from the University of Kentucky—John Wall. Wall has many great attributes as a point guard, but he has a rare talent to go from one end of the court to the other, quickly pivoting in different directions and leaving defenders confused. I believe that, like John Wall, we all can pivot our racing minds to positive and productive pursuits.

One way to pivot our minds and change directions is to be grateful. As you start declaring thanksgiving, you will be sucked out of the negative. Another way of saying this is, "We don't have to be grateful *for* everything that happens to us, but we can be grateful *in everything* that we are going through."[13] By consciously thinking thoughts that promote our personal well-being and empowerment, we can nourish and uplift our lives. This is the true definition of living a successful life.

I've found that successful people frame situations and problems in a way that exudes confidence and success. This is called cognitive repositioning. If the right frame is put around a not-so-pleasant picture, it may look better. The old expression, "You win some and you don't win some, but you never lose!" refers to the fact that it's never a situation itself but our thoughts about it that determine our level of success.

When we incorporate awareness into our days and make the effort to choose positive thoughts over negative ones, we strengthen our minds and their capabilities to serve as solid foundations for our growth, achievements, and dreams. One exercise that has helped me is listening to inspirational worship music. First, this helps me to declare positive words, and second, it helps me to remain peaceful in

---

13   In 1 Thessalonians 5:18 (NIV), Timothy declares, "In everything give thanks; for this is the will of God."

the midst of storms. You can do this, too, with any genre of music, as long as you connect to the lyrics.

# "What If I'm a Pessimist?"

Sure, some people are more naturally prone to sunnier outlooks than others. But none of us should use this as an excuse for a habit of negative thinking. This doesn't serve us, nor does it reflect our lives' plans. This is not to suggest that one forgoes practical or critical thought, though.

We all have negative thought habits that center on guilt, regret, and pessimism, but we can't let them rule us. The question to ask yourself is this: Are you going to continue obsessing over the mistakes you made in the past, or are you going to focus on what can be accomplished in the future?

What takes up space in our minds today takes up space in our lives tomorrow. When we learn from our negative thoughts, we can find the root they stem from and address it to better our future selves. And to see new opportunities before us, we need to have the openness and clarity to accept them. This requires learning from and letting go of the past so we can live in the present.

When negative thinking creeps into my mind space, I like to replace it with Christian scripture, which Daddy Joe always taught (consistent with classical Christian belief) was God's Holy word. I usually contemplate Philippians 4:4 (NIV), which says, "Rejoice in the Lord always. I will say it again: rejoice!" (Or if someone like Taylor Swift is more your cup of tea, "Shake it off!")

Your thoughts affect your emotions, and your emotions affect the choices you make. Your mind is the seat of your power. When you change your thoughts, you ultimately change your life. At the end of the day, it's best to center our minds on gratitude and joy. When we do this, we choose thoughts that propel us toward our goals and ambitions, and our actions follow accordingly.

## What Do You Feed Your Mind?

If you walk into a college football team's locker room, you'll see only positive messaging on the walls, posters with phrases like "Why not us?" or "Start fast and finish strong" or "Play like a champion."

There are no posters hanging in locker rooms that read, "We failed last year" or "Maybe we'll win this time." Coaches and athletes realize the power of the mind, and consequently, they surround themselves with positive messages and ideas. They understand that winning and success require physical and mental preparation. Great athletes (especially quarterbacks and kickers) visualize success. We must do that as well.

Yes, we must do the physical work required to reach our goals, but we can't forget the mental side of the equation. It's just as important to feed our minds healthy thoughts as it is to feed our bodies healthy foods. We must surround ourselves with positive messaging and positive people if we want to realize our highest potential and the powerful purposes and plans for our lives.

> *"For I know the plans I have for you," says the Lord. "They are plans for good and not for disaster, to give you a future and a hope."*
>
> —Jeremiah 29:11, NIV

# Body

A healthy body is the final component of a strong base. Many people, myself included, have found that health is the foundation—the base— for all of life's accomplishments.

Our bodies support every aspect of our existence. It's easy to take them for granted, but they're gifts to us. We need to treat them as we would a BMW or Tesla parked in our garages: with care and respect. If our bodies aren't working, everything else in our life suffers.

## A HOLISTIC APPROACH TO GETTING BACK TO BASICS

Many people cringe at the idea of making healthy lifestyle changes. What will they have to do or (worse) give up? Today's health and weight loss market is flooded with fitness technology, detox diets, and cutting-edge workouts promising to revolutionize our health. All these resources are great tools, but having too many fitness options at our fingertips can be overwhelming.

A healthy lifestyle doesn't have to be a time-consuming trip down self-denial lane. It's not an all-or-nothing venture either. You don't need to work out five hours a day, and you don't need to turn vegan to have an energized and healthy body.

Through Daddy Joe's example, I learned that the easiest and most pleasurable road to health is one that takes us back to the basics. It's the simple actions and habits performed consistently throughout entire lifetimes that support well-being and longevity the most.

Daddy Joe never had a gym membership or participated in juice cleanses. Nevertheless, he lived a robustly healthy life into his nineties. He accomplished this by centering his days on two integral principles: balance and simplicity.

No matter his age, he made time to socialize with his community, read the newspaper, and move his body daily. Even in his seventies, he walked around his neighborhood and delivered eggs to customers, chatting with neighbors every step of the way. I believe he chose simple activities that exercised his body, mind, and spirit because he intuitively understood that a holistic and balanced approach to health is a powerful one.

## THE SEXY BACK METHOD

Please don't chuckle, but sometimes I jump rope at the gym to old Justin Timberlake songs. And while it may be a bit dated, one of his songs underscores my next point. We all want to bring our sexy back. But to do so, we have to work at it. What this means is that we must work toward results. Getting our sexy back doesn't happen by sitting on the couch. Trust me, we've all tried, and we've all failed!

Fortunately, I have health coaches in my family, and they constantly remind me to keep my health routine simple. Inspired by Daddy Joe's example, and to engage readers, I use a basic approach to health called the SEXY Back Method. I even ran this by my doctor and nutritionist. They thought it was cute, but both told me to *just do it!* Like the Nike slogan, my method is all about making the most of your life. The SEXY Back Method serves as a fun reminder to do the following:

**S**tress less—Create a less stressful life by focusing on home, routines, and choices.

**E**at well—Consume fresh, whole foods and nonstarchy vegetables.

**Ex**ercise—Move the body regularly.

**Y**ield to other powers—Accept limitations to your aspirations, and be accountable to the needs of self, family, friends, and the community.

How does it work? First, we must manage our stress levels. We must ensure that our finances, relationships, and work lives are healthy. When it came to finances, Daddy Joe never allowed debt to enter his life. He kept a clean budget and paid for two homes in cash—quite an accomplishment, but still doable in his day. In the modern day and age, that kind of accomplishment can be a tall order for some folks, but you don't have to shoot for the moon. Focus on your values and on reducing your stress accordingly. This could look like creating a calendar of bill due dates, creating a savings plan, or simply looking at your accounts at the beginning and end of each day to keep an eye on your balances. Some folks might want to avoid looking into the numbers out of anxiety, but in my experience, this is one of the best ways to get more comfortable with your finances quickly and relieve some of that stress by having faith in yourself to assess your financial needs and wants appropriately.

When I was thinking of making my first large purchase, I remember Daddy Joe telling me, "Don't overextend yourself, Mark." He was essentially saying, "Don't deplete your energy by making a financial decision that may cause stress." I'll never forget this wisdom. I think a laudable and healthy goal is to strive for a debt-free life. It has the power to improve our health and our relationships. The same logic holds true for the relationships and careers in which we choose to invest. The cleaner and calmer we make our outer lives, the more energy and time we'll have for our priorities and goals.

Daddy Joe and Mother had to be innovative to own their own home and live in the spirit of their generosity. Despite Daddy Joe working two jobs, they were also smart about sacrifices. When I was a young kid, Daddy Joe and Mother bought couches—the ones that Mother still has today! It seems that they immediately decided to cover the couches in plastic zip covers. I'm not sure who came up with this innovation of beautiful, upholstered couches covered in sealed plastic! Anyway, that meant that every time we stayed at their house, the sheets that Mother laid on the couches for us would eventually slip off, and we'd hear each other sticking to and sliding off the plastic couch covering all throughout the night. If it meant sacrificing a couple of nights of comfort, then so be it, because Daddy Joe and Mother were going to keep those couches that they worked hard for and paid for in cash.

When it comes to eating habits, I think the most important principle is moderation. Daddy Joe and Mother didn't deny their cravings, but they never overate or overindulged, allowing moderation to guide their eating habits. They also kept their own version of Whole Foods Market in their backyard: a garden brimming with fresh, organic produce. You may not have the time or resources to maintain a garden, but we can all make an effort to choose fresh produce and whole food sources on a regular basis.

Also, exercise *regularly*. If you love a routine such as going to the gym, attending your favorite kickboxing class, doing core exercises, or attending a CrossFit facility—that's great. If all that sounds unappealing, choose something simple, like taking a walk every day. It doesn't matter how complex or simple we make our workout routines. What matters is that they fit into our lives and are enjoyable. When these two needs are met, exercising is no longer a chore or item on a to-do list; it's a way of life.

Lastly, if we want to work on getting our sexy back, we need to *yield* to the sense of power that we hold over ourselves. This allows us to become stress-free. Yield to thoughts by practicing mindfulness or being present. Yield to others by getting help and maintaining accountability. Yield to your community by giving back (perhaps through volunteerism). We are healthier when we give back and help our community. Yielding provides purpose, accountability, and a reason to get up and move!

# Don't Plant Your Dreams in Cement

Self-care is the foundation necessary to create a fulfilling, passion-driven life. When you prioritize work over self-care—your base—you jeopardize your health. We should reflect on why we do this and seek to reset and change directions.

Without a strong base centered on soul, mind, and body, any efforts to grow a fruitful life will fail. You can't grow your ambitions if you're planting their seeds in cement. Nourishing and caring for the soil that supports your life's fruits must always come first.

A powerful base precedes a powerful life. No exceptions. It's the law of thriving.

To recap, check out the questions and action steps that follow. Remember: this book isn't just a fun read. This book is meant to create change in your life. Change requires action!

# Putting Words into Action: Reflection Questions

Build your base this week. The results are cumulative!

1. Soul

   □ Practice the four P's (pause, pray, peace, praise) for the next seven days.

   □ Journal each day on the changes—inner and outer—that surface as you deepen your practice. What do you notice?

2. Mind

    ☐ Post a positive message on your bathroom mirror or in another prominent place—make it your phone's lock screen, even, so you can see it all the time. Meditate on the message throughout these seven days, then journal on the changes, inner and outer, that surface as you focus your mind on positive, empowering thoughts.

    ☐ Each day, write down something you are grateful for to ingrain it in your mind and recognize new things to be grateful for.

3. Body

    ☐ Incorporate fresh fruits and vegetables into at least one meal each day.

    ☐ Move your body for at least thirty minutes each day.

    ☐ Reflect, then journal on how daily exercise and nutritional awareness affect the way you feel and act. How does taking care of your body support other areas of your life?

    ☐ Set an appointment for a physical checkup, or schedule a meeting with a nutritionist or health group.

# CHAPTER 3
## People Matter

*You and the People You Love*

The Henry family—Daddy Joe's family and mine, though I have a different last name, as he was my maternal grandfather—has had some great reunions during the last few decades. We call them "the Henry Holiday Family Reunions" because Daddy Joe and other leaders in the family taught us to view coming together as a treat, not an obligation. He taught us to approach all relationships with integrity, openness, and respect, because in his eyes, healthy relationships were the foundation of a healthy existence.

Looking back on Daddy Joe's life, it's clear he was blessed with supportive, fulfilling relationships because he made the effort to cultivate them. He and Mother had a true open-door policy—a rare phenomenon these days. His house was a haven in which anyone could stop by and receive both a hearty meal and conversation. Daddy Joe would do the talking while Mother cooked her famous homemade rolls. (I loved those empty carbs.) I have fond memories of him and

Mother sitting on their front porch, a shining twinkle in Daddy Joe's eye as he chatted up whoever came by for a heart-to-heart.

On the subject of open doors, I must mention my wonderful great-aunt, Auntie. Auntie would always have her door open when we came running up the stairs of her duplex. "Come on in here!" she'd holler from inside. She gave tight, strong hugs, and like an old football or basketball coach, she would give you a hard slap on your thigh as a sign of love. We would sit at her table for hours, listening to stories and gaining wisdom. Auntie was tough and always showed love but gave good constructive criticism. If you listened and welcomed it, your life would be better. Auntie and Daddy Joe were brother and sister, and they both lived good, long lives well into their late nineties!

Like his sister, Daddy Joe was generous with his time, food, and home because he understood the rule of generosity: what you give out, you receive back a hundredfold. By dishing out large servings of love, he received even more in return. He also knew how to add a bit of fun to routine tasks.

Every time we drove from Saint Louis to Chicago, we'd all scramble and hop over one another to drive the car into the driveway. This was because Daddy Joe's first greeting was always, "Who drove it all the way in?"

Now it didn't matter that my dad or mom had driven five hours or that we had just hopped in to drive it the last fifteen minutes. We all wanted to be the one to say, "I did, Daddy Joe; I drove it all the way in."

Then Daddy Joe would smile and say, "Go get ya something from the refrigerator." Daddy Joe loved RC Cola. He always had some in the fridge and made sure everybody who came over was welcome to it too. Daddy Joe seemed to also always have duck or turkey in the fridge. I don't know where he always got duck in downtown Chicago.

In hindsight, I think it may have just been chicken that he called duck, but he and Mother always had fresh homemade rolls, duck, and RC Cola that they generously shared with those who came over.

Daddy Joe taught me that positive relationships are integral to feeling spiritually fulfilled in life and that we must invest effort and care into our relationships if we want them to blossom and grow.

# Relationships Are like a Good Game of Football

We can enjoy rich relationships, as Daddy Joe did, by constructing them with wisdom and thoughtfulness. In fact, creating healthy relationships is like playing a winning game of football. Both endeavors require strategy—Daddy Joe knew this very well.

Like a football team needs excellent offensive and defensive plays to execute and win a game, we need a strong set of go-to plays that help us to thrive in our relationships.

We all want to advance our intimacy and healthy boundaries, but these developments don't happen automatically. We need to be smart and strategic about our approach to relationships and disciplined in utilizing the most powerful tools at our disposal.

Having a strong set of offensive and defensive strategies in our game plan is fundamental to cultivating enduring bonds with those we respect and love. Let's start with relationships on the offense.

## PLAYING OFFENSE

For those unfamiliar with football, the offense seeks to advance down the field with the end goal of scoring a touchdown. The quarterback heads the operation. A team's ability to score is contingent on its quarterback being a good leader who can inspire strong performances from his teammates.

There are several great quarterbacks on the field today and in NFL history: Patrick Mahomes, Joe Burrow, Dak Prescott, Josh Allen, Russell Wilson, Kurt Warner, Roger Staubach, Warren Moon, Peyton Manning, Cam Newton, and even the GOAT, Tom Brady, to name a few. These quarterbacks know how to get the best performance from their offensive teammates, which enables them to elevate their teams and ultimately score touchdown after touchdown until they win!

Great quarterbacks score often. They aren't the proverbial ball hogs, who only play to show off and puff up their egos. They understand the value in putting their teammates in the right position to score, both on and off the field. Great quarterbacks deliver while the game clock is running, but the best quarterbacks also lead their teammates in locker rooms, in practices, and in life. This team spirit elevates these players to the top of their game.

Being a great quarterback in our relationships will elevate us to the top of our game as well. Like a good quarterback, we need to be skilled leaders in our relationships. If we use the right set of strategies, we can inspire advancement toward authenticity, openness, and compassion in all our interactions.

# Strategy 1: The Six Most Important Words

A few years ago, I stumbled upon one of the most effective strategies for strong interpersonal relationships. At the time, I had been living and working in Washington, DC, for over a decade. Like in all professional circles, small talk was commonplace. Yet the lack of substance in all these conversations began to exhaust me. One night, I got on my knees and prayed for a road to more meaningful conversation.

After that night, my wife and I visited my old childhood friend Bob and his wife, Susan. After chitchatting for a while, it appeared there was nothing else to be said. I was about to initiate goodbyes when an inner nudge made me pause. Six words suddenly crossed my lips: "How can I pray for you?"

A silence permeated the room. To my surprise, tears welled up in Bob's eyes. He asked me to pray for an ill family member, his and Susan's jobs, and for their newborn daughter. As they shared their concerns, my wife and I revealed our personal struggles as well. We spent another hour in deep conversation, praying for the heartfelt needs of one another. As I left Bob's home, I realized my prayer was answered. He had given me six little words to revolutionize my conversations.

Asking "How can I pray for you?" or "What's going on in your life? How can I support you right now?" is a powerful tool that pushes engagement beyond the surface level to the heart of connection and openness. No one is going to answer the question with, "Well, pray for Derek Jeter because he just retired, and I'm sure he's upset." Instead, you'll hear responses like, "Actually, I'm struggling at work right now, and I'm fearful of the toxic environment" or "My friend has been dealing with a health issue these last two months and it's really taking a toll on his/her family" or "Please pray for my son/daughter who is away at college." Suddenly, the conversation has reached a new level of significance and intimacy. You suddenly become a vessel of hope and behind-the-scenes support.

At the heart of relationships is service. Checking in on each other in meaningful ways offers the most expansive form of service we can give our friends and family.

# Strategy 2: Hope-itosis

Along with service, positivity is integral to healthy relationships. Gossip, unbridled anger, foul language, and even consistent sarcasm can poison what could otherwise be a strong dynamic. These negative forms of speech are akin to halitosis, which is bad breath caused by bacteria. Similarly, negative speech creates a foul, clouded atmosphere that blocks out hope and optimism.

Negative speech is also a tremendous turnoff in any situation. Even during elections or postgame press conferences, we can feel the difference between candidates or coaches attempting to convey positive messages versus belittle others. The latter is limited in power and substance, and it rarely provides useful information.

Ironically, gossip is sometimes used as a tool to bond with others. In the end, though, nothing is as divisive and negative as turning your back on a teammate. A good quarterback knows this move is fatal in a game. It can be fatal to relationships as well.

We can keep such negativity from contaminating our relationships by connecting with our spirits daily and spreading "hope-ito-sis"—the message of hope and enthusiasm for all that life provides.

The next time a negative whisper meets your ear, be the friend that turns halitosis into hope-itosis. If others aren't willing to transform their negativity, then be strong enough to walk away and rise above it.

When we commit to infusing our relationships with hope, we give them healthy, nourishing soil in which they can grow and blossom.

Many thanks to the leaders of the past, present, and future who are spreading *hope*, which we'll talk more about later in the book—we all believe the best is yet to come!

# Strategy 3: The GEL Method

The final strategy is a support-based one that I call the GEL Method. I love to run, and I'm slowly becoming an avid runner. When I started jogging longer distances regularly, I found myself being particular about the kind of shoes I wore. I needed strong support. My favorite kind of shoe is a low-drop running shoe that's equipped with gel cushions—the ultimate protection against aches and pains.

Relationships also need strong cushions to protect against unnecessary pain. We can endow our friendships and partnerships with an extra layer of support by using the GEL Method: a conversation strategy that encourages intentional discussion. I've found that the GEL Method often gives my relationships a "New Balance" (pun intended). It helps us facilitate the key ingredients of substantive dialogue. It's an acrostic that stands for:

**Gratitude—Articulate what you're thankful for.**
**Encouragement—Encourage conversation partners.**
**Life lesson—Give a positive life lesson.**

Imagine you're sharing a Thanksgiving meal with your family. Here is an example of how you can incorporate the GEL Method into conversation to create a meaningful connection with those you love:

Gratitude: "I'm so thankful for this job ..."

Encouragement: "I really appreciate that you ..."

Life lesson: "I'm learning to pause before sending emails. It makes the biggest difference!"

Let's return to the idea of playing offense for a moment. As an example of using the GEL Method offensively, let's say your goal is to lead and empower others through a positive, faith-filled example. You can use GEL when in conversations with coworkers, leaders, family, and friends in this way:

**Gratitude:** *[Name], thank you for ... / I appreciate that / how you ...*
**Encouragement (hope-itosis):** *I hope you ... / I love that you ...*
**Life lesson:** *Did you know ... ?*

Bring the conversation to a close with "How can I pray for you?" The GEL Method is a simple dialogue road map that leads to destinations characterized by quality, optimism, and growth. It's a great tool to have at your disposal during interviews, performance reviews, or even negotiation deals. For example, simply saying, "John, we appreciate your good work," can go a long way in creating a winning company culture.

The more you utilize the GEL Method in your conversations, the more bounce and support you will feel in your relationships and overall life.

# Playing Defense

Now it's time to strengthen your defensive relationship strategies to create healthy boundaries that serve you and those you love.

Two of the greatest defensive players of our time are Ray Lewis (winner of two Super Bowls) and J. J. Watt (an MVP defensive lineman). Both knew how to effectively protect their team. They never walked onto the playing field without a plan and the safeguard of heavy padding and armor. They were both always prepared.

Like Lewis and Watt, we need to armor up with a protective strategy before interacting with others. Conflict is inevitable. However, when we're prepared, we can power through situations, just as Lewis and Watt did out on the field.

## THE KEY DEFENSIVE STRATEGY: POOP

This strategy isn't as smelly as it sounds. I know some people may balk at this and feel that using a scatological reference dilutes the message. There are certainly other naming conventions I could have gone with, but there's a story behind this strategy that's important to understanding why we sometimes have to deal with, well, the poopy parts of life.

Let me set the stage: I grew up in the South and Midwest, where cow tipping was an integral part of high school lore. Colorful stories always floated around lunch tables about teenagers sneaking into fields after late-night parties, mischievously tipping over cows. I don't know if this ever really happened, but the stories were always fun to hear.

Imagine taking part in this late-night adrenaline rush. You drive up to the side of a cow field and hop out of your car. Excitement runs through your blood as you jump the tall fence bordering the field. Suddenly your stomach drops. You realize your party clothing is completely inappropriate attire for plodding around in a cow field. You look down, and to your dismay, your leather loafer is sinking into a big, sticky cow pie. As your shoe sinks farther into the dung, you quickly try to yank it out. Only your foot emerges, leaving your shoe suctioned into the patty. Now you have to hop on one foot, reach down, and pull your shoe out. You're sure it's ruined—and so is your evening.

Being "pulled out of peace" (POOP) can be just as unpleasant as stepping in a sticky cow patty. Encountering POOP in our relationships and personal interactions may be a daily phenomenon: How many times have you wanted to pull your hair out after a run-in with a colleague who always presses your buttons or a call with a family member known for picking fights?

Well, here's the good news: Your day doesn't have to be ruined when conflict surfaces—not if you have the right methods in your relationship tool kit!

## Method 1: Awareness

Lasting peace and satisfaction can't be found in outside situations or people; they must be cultivated within. Awareness is the first step to doing this. We have to be realistic and acknowledge that there are plenty of sticky situations that can drag us out of peace—in other words, that can trigger the least positive and thoughtful parts of ourselves and lead us to make decisions that won't serve us in the long run. However, we can use the power of awareness to help us navigate through the moments when POOP hits the fan and we're feeling triggered.

Awareness functions like a flashlight in a dark cow field. It illuminates the path before us so we can see the piles of drama and avoid them. When we are unaware, we simply react to whatever is transpiring around us. In this mentality, it's easy to get consumed by tension and chaos, like a shoe sucked into a cow pie.

Avoiding reaction to protect our relationships and inner peace requires thoughtful decisions. We must declare each morning that we will maintain our inner peace and joy, no matter what's said or done to us. When we cultivate mindfulness and awareness in uncomfortable situations, we maintain our equilibrium. We see the drama and can choose to sidestep it or walk away. This is because we make the decision to protect our peace, no matter what.

Daddy Joe taught his children and grandchildren that no matter what, whether you've had your coffee or not, you need to declare that it is a good morning. This is a small habit that can make a world of difference. It's like the old saying: "Good Lord, it's morning" versus "Good morning, Lord."

Awareness also means acknowledging our ability to POOP on others—to pull them out of peace. We must be mindful of how our words and actions affect others. When we pause and ask, "Is my response kind? Does it reflect my integrity?" we commit to creating a clean space in which our relationships can thrive.

The more aware we are of POOP, whether we risk stepping in it or creating it, the more power we have to choose peace instead.

When you are taught to drive, the instructor will tell you to focus on where you want the car to go, not where you don't want the car to go. Life works the same way. Let's focus on where we want our lives to go, not the negative ditches or pitfalls. We should make our focus on "staying in peace," not avoiding the POOP. When you get up in the morning, think about how to stay in peace! It is like a great morning coffee or tea—think "SIP": stay in peace!

## Method 2: Table It

When we cultivate awareness in our interactions, we sense with greater acuity when there's a whiff of POOP in our dynamics. Very seldom does being pulled out of peace happen immediately. It's usually a process that builds slowly. Instead of allowing stress to gain momentum, we can take proactive steps to ease tension and prepare for constructive dialogue.

Whether having a conflict with a friend, spouse, or colleague, we can say, "You know, I care about this situation, and I'd like to think about everything you said. Can we finish discussing this tomorrow?"

Tabling heated discussions allows everyone time to cool down and helps us approach the subject with greater objectivity and care.

## Method 3: "L'Eggo My Ego!"

Back in 1972, a silly commercial aired in which a father and son fought over an Eggo waffle popping out of a toaster. Both characters declared, "L'eggo my Eggo!" The slogan stuck, and the ad campaign enjoyed several iterations that lasted for generations.

In times of conflict or drama, there is something more important to let go of: we should let go of having our egos run the show. Unless you want to be pulled out of peace frequently throughout your day, you must leave your ego at the front door every morning. The ego is like a blindfold. If you walk through relationships with your eyes covered, you're going to entangle yourself in conflict after conflict.

Instead of taking this route, ask yourself, "Is protecting my ego worth engaging in this conflict? Can I let my ego go?"

A few weeks ago, I was negotiating a simple business deal. (Unfortunately, I was not on *Shark Tank* pitching Mark Cuban—perhaps one day.) While we were negotiating, I found myself getting very bothered over a small issue. I wanted to win that minor battle more than close the deal. I wanted to win on all counts. Then I heard a voice in my head whisper, "L'eggo your ego, Mark. You don't have to win this." I took a deep breath and cooled down. I then approached the situation from a more detached vantage point, which ultimately worked to everyone's advantage. That little voice was a great reminder to hold true to my intention to maintain my peace.

When you win an argument but lose your peace of mind in the process, you aren't really winning. Time to l'eggo … of that ego!

## Method 4: Forgive about It

The final method for maintaining peace is forgiveness. New Jersey is known for many good things, one of them being the saying "Forget about it" (or for those interested in keeping the accent, *fuhgeddaboudit!*).

I like to use a variation of this phrase—"Forgive about it"—when deciding to remain angry about a past grievance or offer forgiveness.

Daddy Joe often forgave. A great example is the family cross-country trip that I mentioned earlier. When Daddy Joe and the family stopped to use a restroom, Daddy Joe was confronted with prejudice and threatened with violence. He hightailed the family out of there and never looked back. He didn't let the fear or anger stay with him; he felt those feelings and then used them to build his home and create a legacy for his family.

It can be difficult to forgive, but it's a necessary step on the path to inner peace. Harboring resentment and blame toward people or events only harms you in the end. When you let go of anger and bitterness, you release the hold other people's actions have on your life.

In 2014, LeBron James announced that he was going back to the Cleveland Cavaliers. Many saw this as a story about forgiveness. I've encountered situations in which I needed forgiveness from others and in which I needed to extend forgiveness to others. I believe the great city of Cleveland even put up a sign: "Forgiven." (I hope that won't change now that LeBron is with the Lakers!)

To continue with the idea of basketball, throughout your life, there will be times you go "hard to the hole" for a layup and get fouled. I believe that you need to call the foul and acknowledge the hurt—that's how you respect your own boundaries and goals. But you don't need to retaliate. Don't let yourself get blinded by the emotions of being fouled. Take a deep breath, and then make a forgiveness free throw instead. In practicing forgiveness, you can focus on the game in front of you. Call out the fouls of life, but remember to forgive and forge onward. For instance, once a player gets fouled—you see them go to the foul line—they normally take a deep breath and think about making the basket. If the shooter is staring down the other players, or distracted by the crowd loudly chanting her name, she will invariably miss the free throw. Instead, call the foul, take a deep breath, shoot the free throw, and move on to play the game in front of you. For instance, Steph Curry and Caitlin Clark—and many other athletes—exemplify this type of concentration, focus, and forgiveness free throw mentality.

To take POOP on the defense, you can follow this simple strategy we've outlined to protect yourself from negative, unhealthy, and harmful situations (POOP):

1. **Awareness:** *I need to avoid or distance myself from ... [a person, behavior, or environment]*

2. **Table it:** *I'm not ready to deal / move forward with ... [a decision or dilemma]*

3. **L'eggo my ego:** *I need to let go of ...*

4. **Forgive about it:** *I need to forgive ... [person/self] for ...*

Clinging to the past is living in the past. When you're stuck watching reruns of old grievances, there is no space for new episodes— new adventures and experiences—to enter your life. Forgiveness means walking away from the past and looking onward. It allows you to move on to new frontiers of bigger and better opportunities without the weight of the past on your shoulders or clouded judgment. People who plot revenge and keep lists of grievances very seldom have room for creativity and forward thinking. When you forgive, it gives you room to be innovative and to progress in your life. Ultimately, when you make the decision to forgive, you make the decision to be free.

# Temper Your Passion with Compassion

Now that you've added the highest-impact offensive and defensive relationship strategies to your playbook, it's time to tackle the final relationship principle. Buckle your seat belt: you're in for a ride down Compassion Lane.

Many movies and books celebrate Steve Jobs and other CEOs who are icons of success in today's business world. Jobs was a technological maverick and built a tremendous empire through his genius. I have one of his phones and am typing this book on his computer. Although Apple is not a sponsor of this book, it should be noted that Jobs assisted me in writing it because I used his tools and benefited from his technology. But it's also worth noting, according to Walter Isaacson's biography on Jobs,[14] that interpersonal skills posed a challenge for him; it appears chaos often surrounded his relationships, which likely diminished his quality of life (and perhaps the quality of those around him).

Jobs experienced fantastic business and creative success, but did he live a full and successful *life*? I pose this question not to criticize Jobs, but to highlight (and challenge) the way success is measured today and the way we gauge our own success. Is it more appealing to build an empire but live a life fractured by poor relationships and physical health, or to live a long and harmonious life characterized by wellness, joy, and a fulfilling work/life balance? Which option would you choose?

During my time in Washington, DC, I was moved by an example of compassion and humility set by someone who might surprise you: George W. Bush. President Bush famously ran a campaign promising "compassionate conservatism," but I'm not talking about whether his

---

14   Walter Isaacson, *Steve Jobs* (New York: Simon & Schuster, 2011).

administration lived up to that promise.[15] Instead, I'm thinking of an example of compassion on a purely personal level.

A friend once told me a story about Timothy Goeglein, one of President Bush's senior advisors and special assistant to the president. Tim is kind, empathetic, and a good listener—someone whose character had never been called into question. But as we all are at some point or another, he was also busy, and stressed, and capable of making bad decisions. In 2008, Goeglein committed plagiarism in a few unpaid local newspaper columns. When the scandal surfaced, he quickly admitted his wrongdoing and knew he would have to resign.

As he now tells the story, Goeglein sat outside the Oval Office with his resignation letter in hand, rehearsing his words, waiting with dread to be called in to his appointment with the president. News of the scandal broke in the home stretch of election season, so Goeglein knew it was an unwelcome distraction for a chief executive with more pressing issues filling his calendar that day.

When Goeglein finally entered the Oval Office, he could not even begin his pre-rehearsed apology before President Bush preempted it with words of his own: "Tim, I forgive you."

The President then gave his own advisor an embrace as Goeglein wept. They prayed together; the president asked about his kids and bade him farewell with a warm heart of compassion and forgiveness. President Bush—like President Obama, John Danforth, and John Ashcroft—was a leader who could inspire people and win elections. But the tougher measure of character is whether you demonstrate compassion and humility with people outside the view of television cameras.

---

15    I had the honor of serving in the Department of Justice during the Bush administration, under my mentor John Ashcroft. Many thanks to all the presidents who gave me the honor to serve in and during their administrations—numbers 42, 43, 44, and 45. I've included this story because I think it's a powerful story of human relationships, not because I'm advocating any particular politics or public policy.

History will remember President Bush more for standing on the rubble of Ground Zero in New York holding a bullhorn than it will remember him accepting an apology letter. But his character was the backbone that allowed him to be a successful leader. He made plenty of mistakes of his own, but sometimes another test of character involves the humility to accept mistakes from others with compassion and grace instead of bitterness and resentment.

When I feel my drive to succeed overpowering my compassion for others or myself, I pause to ask a similar question: Would I rather be a revered billionaire who lived a challenging relational life or a revered family man like Daddy Joe, who experienced a long life and solid relationships, and enjoyed himself while accumulating success? Even though Daddy Joe wasn't a millionaire, he was wealthy in *life*. At the end of the day, isn't that what we're all striving to achieve? A friend asked the following: Are we traveling on the road toward the city of earthly riches or the more peaceful countryside? Is it simply a matter of personal preference? Is there room for both in our lives? I'm not sure I have the answer.

I'm not proposing that we can't be billionaires and have joyful, fulfilling lives. What I am suggesting is that the road to successful living is one guided by wisdom and balance. Sacrificing relationships in the pursuit of material success only leads to heartbreak. Perhaps the most important lesson Daddy Joe's example can teach us is that living a prosperous life—in the fullest sense of the word—is living a compassionate one.

## The People Matter Principle

For many years as a lawyer, I worked under a man of faith and influence who was a great role model of how to lead a successful, compassion-filled life. He was a US attorney when I began to work for him and eventually became the US deputy attorney general before transitioning to a leadership role for a nationally recognized law firm and then academia.

I'll never forget the time he announced to an office filled with aggressive trial lawyers, "Hey everyone, our goal reflects the principle that people matter." He went on to encourage us as federal prosecutors to treat defendants, defense counsel, judges, colleagues, courthouse staff, and especially our families, with dignity and respect.

*People matter.* This was the principle that guided his high-profile career to the top. When this revelation hit me, my entire perspective of success changed. Compassion and winning aren't mutually exclusive. There my boss was, standing before me, as living proof of the fact.

If our main goal is to only accumulate money, and we care about nothing else, then our passion for riches will recklessly guide our pursuit. We'll be like a driver careening down a road at night with our headlights off. We'll run over countless people and injure ourselves in the process. I believe that together, we can do better!

Supreme Court Justice Neil Gorsuch likes to warn lawyers about the danger of idolizing their careers by pointing them to Robert Bolt's play *A Man for All Seasons.*[16] In a climactic scene in the play (spoiler alert, if that's necessary for a seventy-year-old show), Richard Rich betrays his mentor, Thomas More, by fabricating testimony against More at trial. Afterward, More learns that Thomas Cromwell made Rich the attorney general of Wales in exchange for his perjury against More. At the time, Wales was a relatively poor and insignificant principality within the kingdom. Realizing the deal Rich had struck, More

---

16    Robert Bolt, *A Man for All Seasons* (New York: Vintage Books, 1990).

remarked, "Why, Richard, it does not profit man to gain the world and lose his soul ... But to gain Wales?"

Sometimes we must ask what the "Wales" is in our own life. What riches and accomplishments do we pursue that will seem hollow and underwhelming compared to our sacrifices to reach them? And who, like More, are the people we betray in the process?

It requires more intelligence and sophistication to balance your passion with compassion than it does to drive blindly toward goals, mowing down whoever is in your way. It may not be the easiest choice, but it is the most beneficial.

As a mentor, I encourage those I work with to adopt this long-term perspective and focus on values-based leadership. By staying true to our principles and serving others with gratitude and humility, we can achieve lasting success that goes beyond material gains. Daddy Joe's life is proof that when we lead with our values, we can create a legacy that inspires and uplifts others for generations to come.

Integrating compassion and kindness into your work ethic allows you to pursue success according to the Golden Rule. "Do unto others as you would have them do to you" is the recipe for a success story.

## Lead with Love

The antidote to fear is knowing you are loved.[17] In today's world of heightened fear and anxiety, finding ways to cultivate a heart of gratitude and an environment of love—unconditional love—may help mitigate the fears we face and the anxiety that rises. Expressing unconditional love takes work, but it should become reflexive, like expressing any other emotion. I can't help but think of the

---

17  1 John 4:18 (NKJV): "There is no fear in love; but perfect love casts out fear: because fear involves torment. But he who fears has not been made perfect in love."

*Inside Out* movies[18] as I write this, with their anthropomorphized characters of different emotions. Throughout the first movie, we watch these characters—Joy, Fear, Sadness, Anger, and Disgust—work together to make sure no one emotion is overshadowed too often by another (they learn quickly that things fall apart and get out of hand if they don't!). Joy and Sadness in particular go on a long journey of understanding with one another, exploring how they each make Riley—the human main character—a stronger and more well-rounded person. (The second movie in the franchise introduces four new characters, Anxiety, Envy, Ennui, and Embarrassment. As of this writing, *Inside Out 2* hasn't been released yet, so I'm putting the cart a bit before the horse in saying this, but I would love to see Unconditional Love as a character … maybe Pete Docter will give me a call to help out with the next *Inside Out!*) Living with our internal emotions on the outside—especially when it comes to expressing and showing unconditional love—is the antidote to fear; it makes room for the core values of transparency and vulnerability, which are pillars of any successful relationship.

# Daddy Joe's Secret Formula

Although he never said it out loud, Daddy Joe's formula for a rich and abundant life included rich, abundant relationships. The fullness and zest that characterized his days were products of his healthy relationships—with his faith, himself, his family, and his community.

Building our relationships with mindfulness and wisdom is one of the greatest gifts we can offer ourselves and those around us. Main-

---

18    *Inside Out*, directed by Pete Docter and Ronnie del Carmen (2015; Burbank, CA: Pixar Animation Studios, distributed by Walt Disney Studios Motion Pictures); and *Inside Out 2*, directed by Kelsey Mann (2024; Burbank, CA: Pixar Animation Studios, distributed by Walt Disney Studios Motion Pictures).

taining a relationship isn't a one-stop shop; it's an ongoing enterprise. We can follow Daddy Joe's lead and make it a priority by instilling our actions and speech with hope, forgiveness, and compassion.

Cultivating masterful relationships helps us realize greatness in all areas of our lives and support our loved ones in doing the same.

# Putting Words into Action: Reflection Questions

Reflect on the following questions, and jot down your insights:

- How do relationships fit into my definition of success?

- What type of impacts do I want to have on my family, work environment, community, and the world?

- What kind of legacy do I want to leave behind for later generations?

- Have I ever stepped in POOP? How might I stay in peace, regardless?

## FREEWRITING ACTIVITY

Only we can decide who we are and what we're capable of achieving. When we fail to consciously decide who we are, we diminish our power by allowing others to do it for us. Take a moment to reflect on your vision for your life. Write down your insights!

## A FORGIVENESS RITUAL

Reflect about forgiveness each night this week. Be more specific if you wish: "I forgive my boss. I forgive my partner, parents, friend, etc." Then manifest forgiveness for *yourself*. Consider what actions you can take to make amends.

Reflect on how this ritual makes you feel or change your views. How does offering and receiving forgiveness affect your relationships? Jot your responses down, and refer to them when you need a reminder to forgive.

# CHAPTER 4
# Win with Values

*Creating a Culture of Success*

One of my favorite movies is *Chariots of Fire* (perhaps because I long to run on the beach and splash in water while music plays in the background). The award-winning movie tells the true story of Eric Liddell, a great athlete who ran in the 1924 Olympics.[19] In addition, another inspirational runner was Harold Abrahams. Both were devout and committed. During the movie, Eric discussed his faith and refused to run the heat for the one-hundred-meter race, his best event, when it was scheduled on a Sunday, the Sabbath. His decision appeared foolish to many. They thought Liddell was throwing away his opportunity to be an Olympic gold medalist.

He stood by his decision because he wasn't running for himself. The traditional sense of winning and losing didn't matter to him, since his self-worth didn't depend on a specific outcome. Success, according to his standards, was living a life that honored his faith.

---

19    *Chariots of Fire*, directed by Hugh Hudson (1981; Los Angeles, CA: Warner Bros.).

That year, Liddell won the gold medal and set a world record for the four-hundred-meter, even though it wasn't his top event. He is a winner—in the Olympics and in life—because he honored his principles. His story is an impressive illustration of the greatness that results from maintaining principles and pursuing success.

Also, I want to mention Harold Abrahams's commitment demonstrated in the movie. I and many others were inspired by his determination and passion to run for a higher cause as well.

My favorite line in the movie is when Eric Liddell falls down, and the coach, Sam Mussabini, yells, "Get up, lad, get up!" I sometimes think when I fall or have setbacks, I hear Daddy Joe saying, "Get up, lad, get up!"

## How Do You Define Your Significance?

Let's take a look at our lives. Do we run for ourselves or for something else? Do we live our lives like Liddell and honor our morals in all we do? Or do we find ourselves solely running after goals and accomplishments with the weight of the world on our shoulders, striving to prove our worth through outside accomplishments?

Many of us have succumbed to focusing solely on accomplishments at one point or another in our lives. It's how the world often encourages us to view success and promote productivity. This perspective is detrimental to the fulfillment and satisfaction we're meant to derive from our accomplishments. It pressures us to work harder for outside sources that don't offer the similar freedom, glory, and joy that Liddell experienced while running.

When we find ourselves caught in this mindset, we can choose to pause and reflect. We can remind ourselves that our bosses, titles, or salaries don't define our significance. When we incorporate this realization into our daily life, our self-worth can never be shaken.

I recall when I was in eighth grade on the Sacred Heart basketball team. We had made it to the parish playoffs. We were having a great game as a team, and I may have been leading all scorers by two points (it was eighth grade—don't laugh). The score was tied thirty-five to thirty-five with five seconds left. My schoolmate Mike passed me the ball, and I missed a last-second shot and also got fouled. I went to the free-throw line with a chance to win the game so our team could move on to the next round. I don't recall precisely what happened because either I blacked out or fainted—bottom line, I airballed or missed the shot. I was devastated. It was very difficult to "shake it off," as Taylor Swift would say.

We went on into overtime and ultimately lost the game. At the time, I didn't realize I had many other sports games ahead of me in high school and college. I didn't realize that my self-worth was tied to my faith, my family, and my friends. I realized that one loss does not define you unless you let it.

I've had to remember this principle from eighth grade through-out my life and career. Hopefully, it will help you as you experience losses and setbacks. Don't let your wins or losses define you—find your self-worth in your faith, whatever that looks like for you.

## Creating a Sustainable Culture of Winning

It's common knowledge that winning requires ambition, discipline, and accountability. Our current culture has mastered this type A side of the equation. Yet we've failed to balance it with peace and wisdom.

Our drive and ambition need to be grounded in something greater than greed and egocentrism if we want to enjoy fruitful, fulfilling lives.

As we strive for success, we often encounter pressure. My son's tennis coach frequently reminds his players of Billie Jean King's famous quote: "Pressure is a privilege." King's wisdom suggests that experiencing pressure is a sign that you're doing something meaningful and challenging—it's a privilege reserved for those who have the opportunity to make a difference or achieve greatness. Building on this powerful perspective, I've come to believe that pressure is not just a privilege, but also an opportunity that teaches us to pray. When we face difficult situations, we can choose to put the pressure on God through prayer, trusting in his guidance and strength. This approach allows us to navigate high-stakes moments with grace and faith. Remember, writing down your goals and declaring them in prayer can be a powerful way to align your ambitions with your faith. By doing so, you're not just setting objectives; you're also inviting divine guidance into your journey toward success. Daddy Joe embodied the success of how pressure as privilege can lead you to prayer. The time period he grew up in was very challenging, but he felt it was an honor to build a life for his family in the United States. The pressure he faced, and we all face, is both a pressure and a privilege—that can cause us to reflect or even pray!

When we operate pursuant to our morals—whether our goals are to climb the corporate ladder or to be the next NFL star—we're endowed with a peace that blunts ambition's sharp edges. When we act according to our morals, we will experience victories that bring inner peace and our soul into equilibrium.

I call this type of peace "beautification." One year, my wife and I had the opportunity to travel to Maui, Hawaii, and stay at the wonderful Grand Wailea. The hotel was under renovation when we were there. Instead of simply hanging caution tape, construction warnings, or hazard signs, the hotel posted a sign reading, "Beautification Project in Progress."

That sign reminds me that when life is tough, we can maintain peace by remembering we are works in progress. This beautification, or peace, enables us to remain grounded and serene while pursuing greatness, so we can actually enjoy our life experiences. When we unite our fierce ambition with beautification, our creativity blossoms. We build a space for miraculous growth. This is when our lives really begin to expand.

# Daddy Joe's Success-Happiness Method

If anyone has achieved remarkable feats during a lifetime, it was Daddy Joe. He had a disciplined, determined work ethic, which allowed him to succeed past his humble beginnings. He was the proud owner of two homes, sent his children to great schools, and accrued sizable savings without the help of a 401(k)—all while being an African American man born in the segregated South.

Daddy Joe's life and endeavors remind me of a quote from Jo Ann Jenkins, CEO of AARP. In her book *Disrupt Aging*, she writes, "I decided then and there that I wouldn't be defined by my race, sex, or income. I want people to define me by who I am, not how old I am, and I refuse to allow the old expectations of what I should or should not do at a certain age define what I am going to do."[20]

Daddy Joe embodied these words. In his early twenties, he courageously purchased a home in Mississippi. He never thought he was

---

20 Jo Ann Jenkins, *Disrupt Aging: A Bold New Path to Living Your Best Life at Every Age* (New York City: PublicAffairs, 2016).

too young or didn't have enough money to be an entrepreneur. He also never thought he was too old to take on a big project. Even in his eighties, he undertook major renovations on his home, restoring it and renting it to a young family. I believe Daddy Joe's zest and zeal for life helped him live a long, prosperous life, and I think we can all learn something from that.

Daddy Joe had many dreams, but above all he prized the balance and beautification that came from his faith. Balance and beautification always accompanied his actions and drive to achieve, surrounding all he did with a strong sense of serenity. Daddy Joe also taught me that true success involves hard work and having fun. In fact, fun fuels your work. If you're not enjoying the pursuit of your ambitions, then you're not living the vibrant existence designed for you.

## Clean Up, Go Up: Winning at Its Best

Daddy Joe also knew the power of a clean, organized life. His finances, home, and personal affairs were always in tip-top condition. He taught me that this kind of upkeep is integral to stress-free living—they're what beautification is all about!

It's hard to enjoy life if you're weighed down by debt or a messy, disorganized home. Peace and beautification come from tending to all areas of life, so you are fully supported in all you do. This support frees the mind to focus on goals and personal growth, so winning and success come more easily. It also prevents you from falling into a rut.

When we clean up, our ambitions prosper. When we clear the baggage and organize our life, we make room for creativity and new opportunities—in other words, we make room to level up. I encourage you—when you're feeling down, struggling at work, or lost in your relationships—to do a spring cleaning and organize your affairs. See a financial counselor, see a marriage counselor, spend a weekend throwing out and giving away old clothes, etc. I guarantee that as you declutter and simplify your life, you will lighten up, see new possibilities, and have creative ideas!

## Winning Is a Long-Term Pursuit

Success isn't defined in the moment, but over a lifetime or longer. When you go through hardship or face troubling times, it's easy to focus on the short-term picture and internalize your struggle and pain. It's easy to become bitter and push against injustices or obstacles that arise. How Daddy Joe handled adversity inspires his grandchildren and great-grandchildren and will, I hope, do so for generations to come. This reminds me of the proverbial "banister of heaven"—one day we will all be looking down on our future great-grandkids or loving relatives over the railing that holds us back, and our desire will be to leave them a legacy of health, wealth, and wisdom.

When Daddy Joe was treated unfairly, he turned to prayer, forgiveness, and determination instead of vengeance. When you become vengeful, your anger poisons everything you do. This approach does more harm than good. It stifles your vision and your state of being, and it can even shorten your life. You no longer have your eye on the long-term win; you're completely consumed by the battle of the present moment, regardless of where it might take you.

Daddy Joe could have been vengeful, but it wouldn't have served his overall ambitions or the vision he had for his children, grandchildren, and great-grandchildren. For him, winning wasn't about trampling the oppression he faced in the moment; it was about planting seeds for the life and opportunities he wanted to build for his family. As with any dream, this required focus on the long-term prize.

Like other great leaders of his time, Daddy Joe foresaw that justice would come through mercy and forgiveness. He didn't let the discrimination and adversity he experienced harden his spirit. He knew he and future generations would be the ultimate victors; it was only a matter of time. And time lasts an eternity.

You and I can use the same long-term focus when approaching our goals. When we trust ourselves and keep our eyes on the long-term prize, we're assured victory in the ultimate unfolding of our lives.

Success in its full, vibrant form is living the life we want. We create a winning culture in our lives by committing to our morals in all we do. The bottom line is that we are destined to win when we trust ourselves and draw our self-worth from within.

# The Seasons of Life

As mentioned, I grew up in the Midwest. The great thing about the Midwest is that you get to experience all four distinct seasons of the year. Like the earth, we experience similar changes.

At times, I found myself frustrated with my career, relationships, and even finances. My frustrations subsided as I remembered that in life, we each go through different seasons. As you create a culture of success in your life, family, and workplace, realize that there are seasons that you will go through on the journey. We never get upset with Mother Nature; when it is too cold, too hot, or just right—it is what it is, and we'll just have to adjust.

# The Man in the Arena

As I watch the Super Bowl, I am always curious about who is in the stands. I think there are three types of people in attendance: people who are against the team, people who are for the team, and people who are simply there for themselves. In life it is the same way.

There are people who are for you, people who may be betting short against you (naysayers), and people who are simply for themselves. This is a hard fact of life, but we must not let the coldness of this reality cheapen our perspective of self. In life, you will have people shouting out your past failures, defeats, interceptions, and fumbles. But like Rocky Balboa, you must have the "eye of the tiger" and focus on creating a healthy culture of winning in your life. Don't let the fans in the stands impact your life.

My good friend and Department of Justice trial coach always encouraged us young lawyers to try the tough cases and block out the noise in the stands. President Teddy Roosevelt addressed this concept in his speech "Citizenship in a Republic":[21]

It is not the critic who counts; not the man who points out how the strong man stumbles, or where the doer of deeds could have done them better. The credit belongs to the man who is actually in the arena, whose face is marred by dust and sweat and blood; who strives valiantly; who errs, who comes short again and again, because there is no effort without error and shortcoming; but who does actually strive to do the deeds; who knows great enthusiasms, the great devotions; who spends himself in a worthy cause; who at the best knows in the end the triumph of high achievement, and who at the worst, if he fails, at least fails while daring greatly, so that his place shall never be with those cold and timid souls who neither know victory nor defeat.

---

21   Theodore Roosevelt, "Citizenship in a Republic," speech, Sorbonne, Paris, France, April 23, 1910.

# God Is Your Barista

One last point regarding people and how I avoid being controlled by the need to please them. When I played college football, I hung the following scripture in my locker:

> Whatever work you do, do it with all your heart. Do it for the Lord and not for men. Remember that you will get your reward from the Lord. He will give you what you should receive. You are working for the Lord Christ. (Col. 3:2 –24, NLV)

I needed to remind myself to give 110 percent and let God be my coach and determine whether I got into the game or not. I still use this scripture today as I work in various venues—I try to remember to give 110 percent unto God. He will determine my steps, rewards, and success.

In this way, I let my faith be my barista (sorry, Starbucks). It fills me up in the morning with encouragement. In Washington, DC, you can see two kinds of people with coffee cups: people with empty cups, begging others to fill theirs, and people who joyfully walk out of Starbucks with their cups filled. The people whose cups are filled with creamy, calorie-filled, caffeine-laden goodness are confident. The people whose cups are empty may be at a loss and looking to others to fill their cups—which can seem helpful in the short term.

I believe we should let our spirit be our barista every morning. Let faith fill our souls so we are not heading out into the world, begging for something to fill our cup. Once our cup is full, we must be willing to help those with empty cups, literally and figuratively.

# Putting Words into Action: Reflection Questions

- Describe what "beautification" looks like in your life. Is it a phrase, image, analogy, feeling, action, or experience?

- In what areas of your life do adjustments need to be made? Focus on one area that needs adjustment this week, and take three steps to create positive change.

- What are your long-term and ultimate goals? What's necessary on the road to success? What can be sacrificed? What is a distraction or temptation?

- How can you enjoy and take advantage of this season of your life, career, faith, etc.?

## CLEAN UP; GO UP!

- Quietly connect with your soul for a few moments each day— perhaps with a cup of coffee. Reflect and feel appreciative of your talents, assets, and contributions.

- Reserve a few hours each weekend for the next month to organize and clean cluttered parts of your home and finances. Record the changes and make lists of what needs to be done.

- Identify your personal values. Imagine they are ingredients in a recipe or courses on a menu. Create a life/career plan that is appetizing and nourishing.

# CHAPTER 5
# Be Innovative and Creative!

*God, I'm Open (GIMO)!*

My life and career followed nontraditional paths. I found that it's human nature to want to control the outcomes of situations, opportunities, and relationships that are important to us. When we truly care about something, we often have a specific vision of success in mind.

While it's important to have goals and desires to strive for, in the end, we must trust the process and believe we will have successful lives. Trusting the process means keeping your eyes and your mind open to accept opportunities, even if they may not look like opportunities at first. My family is a bit musical, as you may have guessed, and my son in particular likes to sing and play the piano. His Sunday school song gets a lot of playtime in our house. I have always loved hearing his voice sing, "All I see, right in front of me, are endless possibilities." It's a lyric from a children's worship song, but it exemplifies a lesson for us all in having a mindset of opportunity and faith in trusting the process. This is the final step to living a fruitful, fulfilling life. GIMO (pronounced "gee-mo") is a method that can help us do exactly this. What is GIMO? It's a three-phase process:

"God, I'm obstinate."

"God, I'm open."

"God, I'm obedient."

The first step is acknowledging the truth of the situation: we're all obstinate from time to time. We like having things our way. By admitting this, we can move forward with our commitment to live the life designed for us. This act also moves us into phase two: "God, I'm open."

Declaring, "God, I'm open," is the ultimate form of surrender. By proclaiming this statement, we relinquish our need to control our lives. We can allow the greatest possible outcomes to manifest by remaining open. Living an open life allows our needs, dreams, and desires to be fulfilled in miraculous ways—often bigger and better than anything we could have imagined.

The final phase of GIMO is "God, I'm obedient." I'll note here that this method works just as well if you feel more comfortable with simply the IMO elements. This method is about speaking faith into your reality, faith that everything happens for a reason. For me, I place that faith in God. When we tell God that we're obedient to his will—obedient to the will of the universe—we're putting our complete trust in him, in the belief that the universe has existed for longer than we ever have, and has protected us through it all. This final declaration of the GIMO method means that no matter what opportunities or changes come in our lives, we will act accordingly. Following the GIMO method, or even just the IMO method, helps to further cultivate and deepen our faith. Oftentimes, you hear NFL coaches say that football is a game of inches—which means one play can make a difference. I try to remind myself that obedience to God is a game of inches. If you review the story of David and Goliath, you will see that David had the courage to obey God, and it changed the trajectory of his life.

# The Most Important Declaration

We need to find our inner GIMO. Somewhere inside of all of us is a spirit conducive to adventure and to declaring, "God, I'm open." It's the most important declaration we can make. Moses was GIMO when he led God's people out of Egypt. David, the young shepherd boy, was GIMO when he agreed to fight the giant Goliath. Young first-term senators or successful businessmen were GIMO when they decided to run for president. Daddy Joe was GIMO when he moved from Mississippi to Chicago. I was GIMO when I left my home in Missouri to relocate to Washington, DC.

My first formative GIMO moment was in 1989. I faced difficult odds in high school because I struggled with coursework. My GPA had dropped to 1.9, and my coach, Gary Kornfield, warned that I would not be eligible to play football without a radical transformation.

I faced a crossroads—would I implode under the weight of circumstances, in a panicked need to control my outcomes? Or would I be able to focus on the parts of life that I *could* control? Then something happened: I prayed. I said, "God, I'm open, and I'm obedient, but I need your help."

Before long, I understood what would come next. I needed to redefine my priorities and process. I was not, first and foremost, a football player trying to protect his status as a football player, figuring out what buttons I needed to push to control my destiny and protect my varsity status. On the contrary. I was, first and foremost, a man of faith and integrity, who couldn't let anything take precedence over my relationship with God.

Finding my identity in my faith reminded me of who I am, which in turn, showed me the things I should do. Because of my confidence in that identity, I studied hard—but not just because I was afraid of not playing football. I studied because I wanted to be a good steward of the opportunities I had been given, to build the skills to serve my faith and family and community. Football was no longer the motivation; it was the consequence.

Whether you believe that I learned that lesson from God through prayer, or that my prayer clarified something within me the way meditation would for you, the takeaway was clear. So were the results. My GPA improved to more than a full letter grade to 3.1. This was the GIMO experience that changed my life.[22]

The *St. Louis Post-Dispatch* even published a story about me giving my life over to God. The paper interviewed my coach and asked me about my plans after high school. "People asked me if I want to play college football," the reporter quoted me as saying. "I say, If I do, it's God's will."

Now you might be yelling at your book now, saying, "No kidding, Grider, you studied! You didn't need a spiritual experience or the Dalai Lama to tell you to do that!" But we all need to get our orientation right. GIMO acknowledges that outcomes are downstream from values, priorities, and mindsets. No matter who you are, regardless of your background or circumstance, you can tap into the bring-it-on spirit inside of you. It's your turn to answer your call to personal greatness and declare GIMO for your life.

GIMO is a motto—to receive all that God wants to give you—and to live your life by the phrase "I'm open," is a simple act with

---

22    See Appendix II for a photocopy of the *St. Louis Post-Dispatch* story.

tremendous payoff. When we live our lives in accordance with GIMO, we live in the light of faith. There's no greater fulfillment or level of success than this.

GIMO challenges all of us to open our minds to a new way of thinking, achieving, and living. Relinquishing control over our lives isn't always easy, but it's necessary if we want to move forward with the freedom, beautification, and success.

Here are some strategies and tools to make the process of letting go and declaring GIMO a bit easier.

## Don't Complete God's Sentences

Part of being open is listening to guidance. This means allowing others to speak without interruption. I'm reminded of a hilarious *Seinfeld* episode in which Jerry dates a girl who always finishes his sentences with the wrong phrase. He can never complete a thought, so this woman never gets to know the real Jerry—only her assumptions about him.[23]

How many times do we try to complete sentences? How many times do we try to insert our desires and will into others' statements? I have found that sometimes your heart is filled with dreams, but you're not supposed to move your feet. In other words, just dream—don't micromanage and try to figure out how it will be accomplished!

At some point in our lives, we've all been guilty of this. Perhaps we said, "OK, I'm going to take this job, and I'm going to go from vice president to CEO because this is the definition of winning." Perhaps this is your life's purpose, but perhaps it isn't. Maybe the version of success intended for you is radically different and more fulfilling than

---

23  *"Seinfeld,"* season 5, episode 6, "The Lip Reader," directed by Tom Cherones, aired October 28, 1993, on NBC.

anything you could have ever dreamed. This is why it's so important to take a step back from our desires and reflect. If we want to grow toward true success, we must take the time to truly listen to God's plan for our lives, and act on it accordingly.

## Know Thyself

Perhaps you find it difficult to tune into your life's purpose. Maybe you don't know where to begin. If this is the case, start with yourself. Who were you made to be? What gifts are you meant to bless the world with? To answer these questions, you must have a certain level of self-awareness. As the old Greek aphorism states, "Know thyself."

Imagine you are the ugly duckling of the fairy tale *The Ugly Duckling*. You walk around believing you are the ugliest duck ever born when you're not even a duck. You're a swan, destined to be one of the most beautiful and graceful birds on the planet. Now imagine if the duck were comfortable being satisfied with just being.

It's time we stop comparing ourselves to others. We must live the life uniquely designed for us, trusting that we will grow into unrivaled beauty and grace. Just think of how much pain the little ugly duckling could have avoided had he lived his life by this principle.

During my high school years, I often felt like I was more duck than swan. I sought to please everyone and, in doing so, lost complete touch with who I was made to be. This led to feelings of inadequacy and emptiness, and it prevented me from fulfilling my potential in the classroom and on the field. It was only when I finally returned to my instruction manual—the Bible—that I rediscovered the truth of who I was. Then I forged a new path of understanding and communication through prayer and reflection. This shift altered the course of my life and is the reason I'm sitting at my computer right now, writing this book.

Did I ever see myself authoring books when I was in high school or college? No, probably not. My younger self would have told you that my future was in sports. Had I held on to that version of success and been closed-minded to the future designed for me, my life would have moved in a very different—and frustrating—direction.

We can all avoid this kind of pitfall by taking time to reflect on who we were made to be. Ultimately, our value is not defined by what society thinks of us, but rather the actions we take in pursuit of fulfilling our life's purpose. When we seek to understand the design for our lives, we begin to realize our true potential and worth.

## An Invocation of Hope

When we're open-minded, we summon hope and wonder into our lives. Even with all the unrest and tension in the world, we can continually return to a state of hope by surrendering our fears. By doing so, we can be like Daddy Joe and offer hope and inspiration to those around us.

Let's take a second to talk more about that word—*hope*, the belief that things can and will get better. If our goal is to inspire hope, then it's essential you embody hope yourself. In fact, you won't get very far without it. Hope is what keeps us going, what allows us to reject the voices in our heads that tell us we "can't." In that sense, having hope is a strategy for success. A life without hope would be like a basketball player walking to the free-throw line, only to turn around and aim for the opposite goal. Having hope is what gives direction to your faith—it's not about making the throw, but about making the throw into the hoop right in front of you. Aim for that—aim for hope—and you won't miss the goal. Some of the time, at least. It's easy to say that you're hopeful, but it's another to actually embody hope.

President Obama ran his presidential campaign on hope and the power of *yes, we can*. I have to thank him for his book *The Audacity of Hope* in particular, because embodying hope does require having the audacity to maintain it. That work isn't easy, especially when you make mistakes and bounce off the backboard, as I have many times. Other administrations have served as excellent examples of the audacity of hope as well—I will always be grateful for my time as a White House counsel and getting to see firsthand how leaders across both parties demonstrated this on a daily basis in their focus, drive, and passion for their constituents. From navigating the Great Recession to leading through the COVID-19 lockdowns, they showed up, empowered by hope, and got to work. None of them were perfect—I certainly wasn't—but they *showed up* and had the audacity to keep on hoping for more and better. And when you embody hope, it's activated into action. If there's one last piece of wisdom I can impart, from all that I have learned from Daddy Joe and throughout my career, it's this: *Don't stop showing up and having hope. Practice, practice, practice.*

You've likely heard the story of, or may even remember, the now famous 2002 rant of the Philadelphia 76ers star Allen Iverson on practice: "We talkin' about practice! Not a game—not the game that I go out there and die for and play every game like it's my last. Not the game. We talkin' about *practice*." Now there were a lot of reasons he went on this particular rant that day in 2002, but the message that has remained through the years is how essential practice is to play the game well. Iverson was a key franchise player, and still at press conferences he was being asked not about the game he'd just played, but about how he practiced. In life, you rarely know the moment the ball is in your court at the very same moment it lands in your hand.

Sometimes you might not realize the power and control you hold, or the gravity of the opportunity before you, until after you let go of that ball and the moment's long gone. Intentionally and consistently practicing the habits we've been discussing in this book is how you learn to recognize when you're holding the ball and to trust yourself to shoot the three. The more you practice, the more second nature it becomes. I want to encourage my young readers especially to remember that the aim with these habits is not to be perfect, but to intentionally live your life with a practice mindset. When a basketball player is at practice, they're not afraid to make mistakes—that's what practice is for. In life, we have to learn that we are not going to be perfect, that life is one long practice period. Having this mindset, knowing you are always learning and growing, will allow you to ultimately reach not just your goals, but also to do so with a sense of peace, fulfillment, and flow.

## Don't Let Anxiety Distract You From God's Purpose

After you say "God, I'm open," nobody promises smooth sailing for the rest of your life. Daddy Joe faced more than his share of stressful moments, but he learned how to respond to them with grace and wisdom. I recently recalled these lessons when I watched the movie *Inside Out 2*[24] with my family. The film took me by surprise with its poignance, because while it was a children's movie, it struck a chord familiar to everyone from 8-year-olds to 108-year-olds, from fourth graders to CEOs: managing our emotions, especially our anxiety and worry. Whether it strikes before a big test, a recital, a family issue, a litigation matter, or even a championship sporting event, we all feel fear, worry, and anxiety.

---

24   Kelsey Mann, dir., Inside Out 2 (Emeryville, CA: Pixar Animation Studios, 2024).

For the uninitiated (or those without young children), the *Inside Out* movies are Pixar animated films depicting a teenage girl's core emotions as individual personified characters. Joy, Anger, Anxiety, Fear, and their friends exist as cute, animated figures living inside the head of 13-year-old Riley, battling for control of the buttons and levers dictating her daily decisions. In one climactic scene— I'll warn you to skip ahead if you are concerned about spoiling an animated children's movie—Anxiety is spinning around in a feverish circle, thinking it is fixing a problem and making progress. Finally, Joy "breaks through" and says to Anxiety, "You need to let her go." These comforting words and presence slow and calm the control Anxiety exercised over Riley's emotions.

Later, Anxiety apologizes to Joy—and they allow Riley to sort through all of her emotions on her own. Riley's friends come over and ask if she's okay and Riley (like us) chooses to apologize and tries to reconcile.

This is a powerful scene because it reminds all of us that we need friends, accountability partners, and our own Joy and Peace to "break through." It also reminds us that when we're spinning, we may need to "let go" of the thing that's causing so much stress—we can slow down, calm our hearts, and breathe.

When I think about this scene, it almost brings me to tears. I think about my life and the lives of others. We can get so fixated on doing well that we stop doing good. There are times when I get wrapped around the axle, and I need my family (i.e. my Joy and Peace) to "break through," slow me down, and say, "Grider—let it go, let it go." But we cannot only always be on the receiving end of generosity. At times, we also need to be "Joy and Peace" for others and encourage them to let it go!

When I start worrying, spinning, and letting Anxiety wrestle away control of my life I think about the Bible verse in Philippians that I break down into a six-to-seven-point strategy to combat fear and anxiety:

1. Don't worry about anything (or at least, don't hold onto your worries);

2. Instead, pray about everything (turn your cares into prayers);

3. Tell God what you need (don't be afraid to ask for a miracle);

4. Thank Him for all He has done (remain grateful amid hardship);

5. Then you will experience God's peace (there's a relief in catharsis);

6. Think about things that are excellent and worthy of praise (try to focus on the good);

Unfortunately for me, I must follow the sage advice from popular shampoo bottles:

7. Rinse and repeat—daily!

# Join Me on the Journey

Putting these concepts on paper has been a rewarding process. Thank you for joining me on this journey of reflection, hope, and discovery. I believe the best is yet to come, as we deepen our commitment to living lives pursuant to strong principles from the base up.

As Daddy Joe's life illustrates, when we pursue success from a spiritual perspective, we set our lives up for achievement and fulfillment that can be passed on for generations. By adhering to these principles, we can leave a legacy defined by virtue, ambition, and accomplishment.

## Putting Words into Action: Reflection Questions

- What decisions or changes am I avoiding? Am I obstinately holding on to unhealthy behaviors, false assumptions, or self-gratifying beliefs?

- What causes me to doubt my trust in myself? Who or what supports and nourishes this trust?

- WITUS—"What is the universe saying?" Take a moment to sit in silence or take a meditative walk. Listen for the inner voice. What is it calling you to do?

- Complete a personality assessment or spend some time in self-reflection. How well do you know yourself?

- Commit to writing out the thoughts, ideas, and inspirations that come to you as you pray or meditate.

- Interested readers can complete the thirty-day journal in Appendix I, which lists Bible verses quoted in this book and others related to the chapters' themes.

# C O N C L U S I O N

## *Who's Your Daddy ... Joe?*

We all have family members, friends, and bosses who have inspired us. Write something thoughtful and encouraging about your "Daddy Joe." Perhaps send the note off to them, expressing your gratitude for their positive presence in your life.

We all have grandparents and great-grandparents who succeeded against the odds—overcame the Holocaust, journeyed to Ellis Island with nothing, led their tribes to success. As you think about your Daddy Joe, they will inspire you to lead. I will never forget the former US senator who met me and said, "Mark, you are a leader." That moment of encouragement continually fuels my ambition to become the kindest and most successful version of myself. I want to leave you with the same declaration and words of encouragement: *you are a leader*. When in doubt, feel free to reach out to me or access supplemental materials on my website, www.markgrider.com. But you can also always return to the twelve key lessons of this book:

1. Be a Soul Man … like Daddy Joe! (Run for the Glory of God)

2. It's All about That Base (Self-Care Is the Foundation)

3. The Real Trifecta: Faith, Perseverance, Humility

4. Temper Your Passion with Compassion (People Matter)

5. Four P's: Pause, Pray, Peace, Praise (Slow Down)

6. Clean Up; Go Up! (Organization + Preparation = Elevation)

7. Don't Step in POOP (Stay/Stand in Peace)

8. L'eggo Your Ego!

9. Hope-itosis (Speak Hope into People's Lives)

10. The Six Most Important Words: How Can I Pray for You?

11. Forgive about It (and Let It Go)

12. Declare GIMO: God, I'm Open! (Don't Complete God's Sentences)

As you embark on your own journey of personal growth and leadership, remember the importance of self-reflection and consider the legacy you want to leave behind. By leading with gratitude, humility, and a commitment to serving others—leading with values—you can create a life of purpose and meaning, just as Daddy Joe did. As a mentor and lawyer, I've seen the transformative power of values-based leadership firsthand, and I encourage you to embrace these principles in your own life and career. We may not be perfect, but with help, we can summon the power to rise to greatness and eventually become someone's Daddy Joe. That is our legacy. May God bless us all with such a calling!

Warmly,
Mark

# APPENDIX I

## *Thirty Days with Godly Words*

There are thirty-one chapters in the Book of Proverbs—one for each day of the month! The best advice I've ever received was to read one Proverbs chapter a day, and I recommend it for you, too, as an exercise in faith, even if you aren't particularly religious—there's something for everyone. And when I say there's something for everyone, I mean it! In fact, my next book may be about applying the principles of jiujitsu and the lessons of Psalms 37 to learn how to fight with faith and win in life. You don't have to be religious to find value in applying biblical teachings in your day-to-day life, the same way you don't have to know jiujitsu to appreciate the skillful art of its combat techniques. Daddy Joe prayed and walked with God every day. To follow in his footsteps, start with the Bible. It's God's Word to us, chock-full of spiritual goodness. Spend time with a different verse each day, and write down whatever comes to mind, how God might be calling you. Below are my own favorite quotes from these verses, which are all NIV unless noted otherwise, and all of which I think have something to offer anyone and everyone, regardless of your spiritual beliefs.

- Trust in the Lord and do good (Ps. 37:3).

- Ask where the good way is, and walk in it (Jer. 6:16).

- He who wins souls is wise (Prov. 11:3, NKJV).

- He restores my soul; He leads me in paths of righteousness (Ps. 23:3).

- Humble yourselves before the Lord, and He will lift you up (James 4:10).

- Stand firm in the one Spirit, striving together as one for the faith (Phil. 1:27).

- Those who hope in the Lord will renew their strength. They will soar on wings like eagles; they will run and not grow weary, they will walk and not be faint (Isa. 40:31).

- Do to others what you would have them do to you (Matt. 7:12).

- In everything give thanks; for this is the will of God (1 Thess. 5:18, NKJV).

- Rejoice in the Lord always. I will say it again: Rejoice! (Phil. 4:4).

- "For I know the plans I have for you," declares the Lord, "plans to prosper you and not to harm you, plans to give you hope and a future" (Jer. 29:11).

- Be joyful in hope, patient in affliction, faithful in prayer (Rom. 12:12).

- We want each of you to show this same diligence to the very end, so that what you hope for may be fully realized (Heb. 6:11).

- In peace I will lie down and sleep, for you alone, Lord, make me dwell in safety (Ps. 4:8).

- Peace I leave with you; my peace I give you … Do not let your hearts be troubled and do not be afraid (John 14:27).

- If you hold anything against anyone, forgive them, so that your Father in heaven may forgive you (Mark 11:25).

- Forgive us our trespasses, as we forgive those who trespass against us *(Our Father* / Lord's Prayer, Matt. 6:12).

- Blessed are the merciful, for they will be shown mercy (Matt. 5:7).

- Father, forgive them, for they do not know what they are doing (Luke 23:34).

- What good is it for someone to gain the whole world, yet forfeit their soul? (Mark 8:36).

- The Lord, before whom I have walked faithfully, will … make your journey a success (Gen. 24:40).

- Keep this Book of the Law always on your lips; meditate on it day and night … Then you will be prosperous and successful (Josh. 1:8).

- Let us run with perseverance the race marked out for us, fixing our eyes on Jesus (Heb. 12:1–2).

- Love the Lord your God with all your heart and with all your soul and with all your mind and with all your strength (Mark 12:30).

- There is a time for everything, and a season for every activity under the heavens (Eccles. 3:1).

- Whatever you do, work at it with all your heart, as working for the Lord, not for human masters (Col. 3:23).

- You make known to me the path of life; you will fill me with joy in your presence (Ps. 16:11).

- May your will be done (Matt. 26:42).

- Your kingdom come, Your will be done *(Our Father* / Lord's Prayer, Matt. 6:10).

- I am the Lord's servant ... May your word to me be fulfilled (Luke 1:38).

# APPENDIX II

## METRO SPORTS

St. Louis Post-Dispatch

MONDAY, AUGUST 28, 1989

FOOTBALL

# SLUH's Grider Makes The Grade

### Faith Helps Junior Billiken On Field And In Classroom

St. Louis University High senior running back/defensive back Mark Grider gives a young team a degree of experience.

*Figure 1: The St. Louis Post-Dispatch article mentioned in chapter 5 about my high school football career in 1989. One of my first and biggest GIMO moments!*

*Figure 2: Daddy Joe at his home, 2121 South Millard*

*Figure 3: Daddy Joe (with an RC Cola!), Mother, and Auntie in the living room at 2121 South Millard*

# ABOUT THE AUTHOR

Mark Alex Grider, Esq., is the grandson of Reverend Joseph Albert Henry (April 1915–June 2005)—affectionately called Daddy Joe. Daddy Joe, a Southern and godly gentleman, inspired Mark to realize his potential, whether it was in business, law, the classroom, or sports. Daddy Joe and the rest of Mark Grider's family helped him realize that he could make the biggest difference by helping and serving others, so he chose to pursue a career in law, business, and policy.

Following law school, a prominent Missouri senator and statesman encouraged Mark to start his career in Washington, DC. In 1998, Mark began serving as a legislative aide and assistant for Senator John Ashcroft. Later, at the Department of Justice, he handled both internal corporate and congressional investigations and currently advises clients on government investigations, civil litigation, crisis management matters, cyber issues, and corporate compliance. Mark has served in multiple administrations, working in the Deputy Attorney General's Office at the Department of Justice, senior associate counsel in the Office of the White House Counsel, and as Deputy Associate Attorney General for two different presidents. During this time, Mark advised key members of the administration on important matters in Congress, the White House, Health and Human Services, and other federal agencies.

Currently, Mark is a partner and Chair of the Litigation, Government Response and Crisis Management team at a national law firm in Washington, DC. He draws on his experience with the US Department of Justice as a former deputy associate attorney general, an assistant US attorney, a senior counsel to the deputy attorney general, and a federal agency deputy general counsel, as well as deputy compliance officer for a Fortune 500 company. He was formerly the executive director of the DOJ's Task Force on Intellectual Property, where he worked on IP, forensics, technology, and cybersecurity policy matters. Grider worked in both chambers of Congress on matters concerning the Middle East and other significant policy issues and served on a high-profile Select Committee on Capitol Hill.

Throughout his career, Mark has been committed to values-based leadership and mentorship. His passion lies in mentoring young leaders, including young lawyers at his firm, inspiring them to live up to their potential the way many senators and corporate executives inspired and mentored Mark. As he serves his team, he attempts to demonstrate the values of leading with gratitude, humility, compassion, and a focus on serving others, just as his grandfather, Daddy Joe, exemplified in his own life. Mark does all of this while capturing the will to win in life and for customers and clients!

In his free time, you'll find Mark spending time with his wife and son, coaching basketball, jogging very slowly, or reading on the porch. Mark attributes his practicing faith and desire to love his family, and he is working to remain true to his values, as he has built his career with compassion and compliance at its core.

www.ingramcontent.com/pod-product-compliance
Lightning Source LLC
Chambersburg PA
CBHW020208090426
42734CB00008B/985